PRAISE FOR
FAIL-PROOF YOUR BUSINESS
and
PAUL E. ADAMS

An easy-to-read checklist for any entrepreneur. Concise and realistic.
—Peter Meehan
Director, Newman's Own Organics

Paul Adams has created a valuable guide for any entrepreneur. Full of sound counsel, wisdom and clear guidelines, it's easy to navigate and is organized in a reader-friendly format.
—Dr. Louis Lataif
Dean, School of Management
Boston University

Great book—insightful, valuable information. I particularly liked the "Remember" comments at the end of each chapter. Wish I would have had it when I was starting my business.
—Herb Myers
CEO, Boxlight Corporation
1998 *Inc. 500* Hall of Fame

Fail-Proof Your Business combines wonderful stories with real-life advice and wisdom to help your business succeed.
—Paul and Sarah Edwards
Co-Authors of *Making Money in Cyberspace* and *Getting Business to Come to You* (Tarcher/Putnam)

more

If we had read *Fail-Proof Your Business* when we started RE/COM, it would have saved us five years of trial-and-error because we would have been better able to recognize and avoid the pitfalls of entrepreneurship. If you are thinking of starting your own business and want to be successful, then take the time to read this book. The reward is well worth the investment.
—**Paul Ferraro, Eric Williams** and **Bernie Mikula**
Partners of The RE/COM Group, Inc., winners of the *Entrepreneur Magazine*/Office Depot 1998 Small-Business Owner's Award

Be prepared for no-nonsense, practical business strategies to help new and existing business persons succeed/survive. Carefully study the excellent chapters on selling, salesmanship and motivating your sales persons—they are exceptional.
—**Dolores Ratcliffe**
President of Corita Communications, Inc.
Founder/President of the Association of Black Women Entrepreneurs

Filled with time-honored, real-world examples that can help you and your business survive and thrive.
—**John Knowlton**
Editor, *Business@Home* (http://www.gohome.com)

Great common and business sense!
—**Nancy Fleming, CPA**

Fail-Proof Your Business tells it like it really is.
—**Professor Edward Moldt**
Director, John Pappajohn Entrepreneurial Center
University of Iowa

The tips in Paul Adams's book will help entrepreneurs avoid mistakes and help ensure a successful business. I wish I had Paul's insight and guidance when I started my catalog company 48 years ago.
—**Lillian Vernon**
Founder and Chief Executive Officer of Lillian Vernon Corporation

Preventative medicine for those who wish to avoid business calamities that are as frequent and likely as the common cold. Easy to read, easy to understand, easy to implement.
—**Brett Kingstone**
Founder and CEO Super Vision International, Inc. (manufacturer of fiber optic lighting and signage)
Author of *The Student Entrepreneur's Guide* (McGraw-Hill) and *The Dynamos* (John Wiley & Sons)

Professor Adams is on the mark. Success in business is not a function of doing the right thing; rather, it is a function of not doing the wrong thing. In today's fast-paced business world, knowing what not to do is very valuable and that is the focus of this book.
—**Marlow Christensen, Ph.D.**
Assistant Professor of Entrepreneurial Studies, Fairleigh Dickinson University

This is solid, down-to-earth advice and answers for anyone planning a new business or experiencing the pangs of grief associated with being "lost" in the excitement of an existing business.
—**Stephen Caplan**
President, KBM Workspace (business-to-business furniture sales)

more

This book is right-on! *Fail-Proof Your Business* will be immensely valuable to entrepreneurs starting a business as well as those trying to grow their business to the next level. *Fail-Proof Your Business* will save you time and money and will be one of the most useful business books at your side. Paul Adams has captured a wealth of entrepreneurial experiences and knowledge that will provide a strong business vision for entrepreneurs and small business owners.
—Brien Biondi
Executive Director, Young Entrepreneurs' Organization

Dr. Adams uses clear language, with easy-to-read, believable examples and simple yet profound suggestions for success. The checklists at the end of each chapter are priceless!
—Dr. Robert A. Scott
President, Ramapo College of New Jersey
Chairman and Secretary, American Educational
Products, Inc. (NASDAQ)

Adams clearly and concisely debunks common myths about emergent businesses. His approach is to take possible failures through practical problem solving and show usable solutions. Selling section is strong.
—William H. Crookston, Ph.D.
Certified Marketing Executive
Associate Professor, USC's Marshall School of Business with the Lloyd Greif Center for Entrepreneurial Studies
Former board member of the International Sales and Marketing Executives Association

Adams offers valuable entrepreneurial insights learned from his personal experiences of what can go wrong and right in starting and operating a new venture. His words of caution and advice of how to reduce risk and what causes failure will force you to stop, think and plan before taking the entrepreneurial plunge so you can experience success.
—**Courtney Price**
Founder and Chairman, FastTrac Entrepreneurial Education Foundation

A superb road-map for achieving long-term success as a small business owner. With 80 percent of new businesses failing, use *Fail-Proof Your Business* to get the odds in your favor.
—**Richard A. Henderson**
Publisher, *HOME BUSINESS® Magazine*

This is an excellent "real world" book on starting a business. While I was ready for another "educator" trying to tell people how to start a business, I found myself saying "finally, a book that passes by the fluff and puts into print what it's really like to start a business.

When I first looked at the cover of *Fail-Proof Your Business* by Paul Adams, my first thought was "just another book filled with big business theory attempting to tell budding entrepreneurs how to become the next Microsoft." But to my pleasant surprise, *Fail-Proof Your Business* was a common sense, grassroots book for the person who wants to start a service business off the kitchen table. It's a book written without the fluff of theory—just the real-world facts.

more

Not too many books start out telling you that 80 percent of start-up businesses fail and that much of what aspiring entrepreneurs hear is more wishful thinking than fact. In fact, the way Adams starts off just might make you want to put the book back on the shelf and forego starting your own business. But that's what Paul Adams does in *Fail-Proof Your Business*. If more people read this book before they took the entrepreneurial leap, there might be fewer people failing in business at the cost of everything they have socked away for a rainy day.

Paul Adams takes the complex theories of building a successful business and boils it down into common sense, understandable terms.

No one goes into business to fail, yet every year hundreds of thousands of people fail to achieve the great American Dream. My guess is that most of them didn't understand what they were getting into. They didn't understand the basic success concepts Paul Adams explains in *Fail-Proof Your Business*.

—**Bennie L. Thayer**
President, National Association for the Self-Employed (NASE)

A quick preview of *Fail-Proof Your Business*

More Americans today are starting a business—be they young people looking for the "opportunity of a lifetime," out-of-work corporate managers seeking salvation or couples creating an "in-home" business to make ends meet. All are enthusiastic and optimistic, but most are unaware of the overwhelming odds of failure: 80 percent of all new businesses fail.

Author Paul E. Adams shows it is possible to beat the odds against failure by avoiding the mistakes of most new business owners. Adams's book fills a much-needed void and is essential reading before anyone risks their life's savings or plunges deeply into debt.

Written in an easy-to-read, common-sense style, *Fail-Proof Your Business* reveals how to stay in business and be successful through such topics as:

- understanding the psychology of failure and success
- mastering money management
- developing essential entrepreneurial leadership skills
- applying successful sales and marketing techniques
- saving a business that's already in trouble
- tapping into special, overlooked strategies for success

Avoiding failure is the other side of the success coin. Adams shows how to pay attention to the warning signs that successful business owners know all about. It's easy to start a business; readers will discover how to stay in business in this accessible, yet comprehensive guide.

FAIL-PROOF YOUR BUSINESS
Beat the Odds and Be Successful

Paul E. Adams

Adams-Hall Publishing
Los Angeles

Library of Congress Cataloging-in-Publication Data
Adams, Paul E.
Fail-Proof Your Business: Beat the Odds and Be Successful
p. cm. Includes index
ISBN 0-944708-56-0 (softcover)
1. Success in business. 2. Entrepreneurship 3. Business failures. I. Title
HF5386.A5134   1999
650.1—dc21   98-43249
                                                   CIP

Adams-Hall books are available at special, quantity discounts for bulk purchases for sales promotions, premiums, fund-raising or educational use. For details, contact: Special Sales Director, Adams-Hall Publishing, PO Box 491002, Los Angeles, CA 90049-1002
AdamsHallP@aol.com or 1/800-888-4452

Cover design by Hespenheide Design
Front cover illustration by Bob Greisen

Printed and manufactured in the United States of America
20 19 18 17 16 15 14 13 12 11 10 9 8 7 6 5 4 3 2

I doubt if I would have finished this book if it had not been for the encouragement and gentle persuasion of my wife Irene, who believing in it from the beginning, frequently asked me: "When are you going to finish your book?" I guess we all need a bit of nagging at times. I doubt if I would have known how to present my draft to a publisher were it not for my friend Marty Fox— an editor, playwright and reporter—who offered his advice and direction. Fortunately, I was wise enough to listen to him. And I want to give a special acknowledgment to my publisher and editor Don Silver who challenged me with the bait of a contract to finish the book on a deadline and who nurtured and guided me through the rewrite and revision process until the final product was created. Without these three very special people, I doubt if *Fail-Proof Your Business* would have been a reality. I shall be forever grateful.

Contents

CONTENTS

CONTENTS

CONTENTS

CONTENTS

Introduction:
Why I wrote this book and
why you need to read it

I considered writing this book for many years but did nothing about it. Semi-retirement has taken away my excuses. As an entrepreneur and business professor, I have always been concerned that most books on entrepreneurship were written by promoters or professors who have never started or operated a business; yet they offer advice and suggestions encouraging people to invest their life savings without any warning of the dangers of failure.

The advice usually consists of the following: get an idea, develop a business plan, borrow money, open the doors and then off you go to being an entrepreneur. Even our federal government is offering advice and encouragement and promoting entrepreneurship as a way of solving some of our inner city problems or addressing the challenge of downsizing. It strikes me as strange that government bureaucrats, sheltered from the marketplace, are offering advice about starting a business.

In our colleges and universities, the majority of business courses are taught by full-time faculty who have little, if any, actual business experience. I question whether secure, tenured faculty are the best qualified to address entrepreneurship. Usually it is the part-time, adjunct professors who teach in the evening that bring the real world experience into the classroom.

In my research, I have found little published information on the real-life problems of business failure—especially small business failure. Yet most new small businesses do fail. If you do a literature search on the Internet or at any major library, you will find plenty of material on small business management and entrepreneurship but little on failure.

Do not get the impression I am against starting a business, because I am not.

I started a sales and marketing agency in the record business (the company was sold to a well-known record producer) and an audio cassette manufacturing and distributing company specializing in the government market (the company is 18 years old and still growing). I also own a small investment company that has a 50 percent interest in a four-store chain selling paint spraying and pressure washer equipment.

From a "hands-on" approach to business problems, I am well-versed in what can go wrong—and right. I have enjoyed success and felt the pain and fear of near failure.

What disturbs me is the blind-faith encouragement to launch a venture without considering the very distinct possibility of failure and without learning ways to prevent failure.

Unfortunately, with failure the norm, too few would-be business owners consider the ramifications of failure and the slight chance of success as they blindly pursue what may be an unrealistic dream.

INTRODUCTION

An example of what I consider bad advice to the owner(s) of a start-up business is the encouragement to borrow heavily through the Small Business Administration (SBA). I know many will disagree with me, but anyone borrowing through the SBA must personally guarantee the debt, which raises the risk if you fail. You could not only lose your investment but everything you pledged, which often includes your home.

This book will show you not only how to fail-proof your business but how to make it a successful one, too. If you take your savings, home equity or pension money, or you borrow heavily to buy or start some enterprise to improve your lifestyle and lose it all, it could very well be a tragedy for you. This book is about the steps you should take to protect your resources.

I have taken a non-academic, common-sense approach. Think of this book not as advice but rather as a series of vital warnings and suggestions by a veteran entrepreneur.

And as a retired professor who taught entrepreneurship, small business marketing and economics for over 25 years, I expect to upset a few of my colleagues with this book. But that is okay.

My purpose with this unorthodox approach to entrepreneurship is two-fold: (1) to persuade the exceedingly optimistic, would-be entrepreneur to be cautious, to be aware and to be alert to the distinct possibility of failure and (2) to help ensure an entrepreneur's success now and down the road.

In the stories and examples used in this book, all names of persons, businesses, cities and states have been changed for privacy reasons.

INTRODUCTION

I sincerely believe the time you invest in reading this book may change the course of your business for the better.

Dr. Paul E. Adams
Entrepreneur
Professor Emeritus, Ramapo College of New Jersey
November, 1998

PART ONE
Understanding the psychology of failure and success

For a business to be successful, the first step is to avoid failure.

How many enthusiastic, optimistic and eager individuals about to launch a new business know or will even believe that eight out of 10 new business ventures fail and only two out of 100 new businesses become successful enough to earn any real money?

In addition, a majority of start-up business failures are caused by the actions or inaction of the owners. To what extent these failures are due to the inborn personality traits or characteristics or subconscious motivations are factors anyone considering risking savings or borrowed money to start a business should seriously consider.

Depending upon the amount of money invested and the age of the entrepreneur, a business failure may be a bump in the road or a catastrophe. If you are middle-aged or a retiree and commit all your resources, such as your pension and the family home, and then fail—that failure may leave you without time or money left to recover or try again.

It is a wise individual who determines in advance if he or she can absorb a failure, recover and go on.

Roger knows this. Shortly after his fiftieth birthday, he launched his dream venture. To do so he cashed in his pension funds and obtained a second mortgage on his home. Unfortunately for Roger, his business failed and today Roger and his wife are renting a small, one-bedroom apartment. He is working as a salesperson for a local autoparts distributor. In three years he will be sixty-five with only his Social Security to retire on.

It is so important for entrepreneurs to understand the psychology of failure—its causes and its consequences. One cause could be a fear of success. Another cause could result from impulsiveness to venture into business with too little regard to the consequences of failure. It is a wise individual who discovers the personality pitfalls preventing success and takes corrective action to turn possible failure into actual success.

Recognize that the failure of a business is far reaching and touches many people: employees who lost their jobs, suppliers of goods and services that extended credit, investors who hoped to make a profit, and of course, the most dramatically affected—entrepreneurs and their loved ones.

Many former owners of defunct businesses will struggle for years following the disaster in debt to creditors, lenders and the Internal Revenue Service. Many will have lost not only their business but their homes and personal possessions as well as their savings.

Perhaps even more upsetting to the failed entrepreneur will be the possible disruption of a marriage, the loss of self-confidence and the general sense of failure as an individual.

If the odds are so much against success, why do so many throw caution to the wind and rush to risk everything in the hope of scoring big? Just turn on the TV or open a newspaper to get the answer. We see and read about fame and fortune every day. We are told this is the age of the entrepreneur (and of many career changes) and we are reminded of the riches that await us if we succeed. But we only know the success stories; the business failures are not presented to us as examples to avoid.

In fact, business failure is rarely discussed or written about unless it is a major company with thousands of stockholders and employees. The small manufacturing company with 10 employees that fails is of little consequence, except to those directly affected. If this is the age of the entrepreneur, it is best not to focus on a failure but to consider only the winners lest you frighten away eager and potential new business owners.

Perhaps, entrepreneurs of failed businesses might have been more cautious if they had realized the risk factor. No one goes into business with the thought of failure. Auto accidents happen to other people, and our friends lose their jobs, not us.

If the possibility of failure is so common, does it not make sense to understand why so many business start-ups never make it beyond the second year of existence? I think so.

Ask an entrepreneur why a business failed and you will nearly always hear: "It wasn't my fault. It was external forces, the market conditions, the competition and the lending policies of the banks that were the cause."

The truth is that personality problems of the entrepreneur are most frequently the cause of failure, not external economic forces. The alarming rate of small business failures in the United States can ultimately be traced to one main cause—ineffective management.

Would-be entrepreneurs bring to their new organizations their personality and character, with all their respective strengths, problems and weaknesses. If an individual is disorganized in life, for example, that disorganization will carry over to the business. Poor personal habits will become poor business habits. The lack of discipline in daily living will lead to an undisciplined management style. Procrastination at home will translate to procrastination on the job. As psychologists point out, wherever we go, we take ourselves, with all our baggage.

Let's explore further how personality pitfalls relate to the psychology of failure.

Chapter 1
Failure and personality

To avoid failing in business, start by understanding yourself.
Question why you are going into business. What are your
motives? Why are you willing to risk your money? Are your
business goals rational plans or emotional dreams?

Self-awareness, self-knowledge and a clear understanding of
your strengths and weaknesses will be important to your success.

Problems and pressures from employees, customers and vendors
require emotional resiliency and a stable personality. If you are
aware of your personal limitations, you can work to avoid
placing yourself in situations that are too difficult for you to
handle.

To thine own self be true
Self-awareness and self-understanding are not easy. Many people
spend a lot of time in therapy seeking their inner self. If we do
not know who we are, have little understanding of our talents or
if we live in a fantasy world with unrealistic goals, how can we
succeed in starting a business that's full of challenges?

Self-honesty and awareness mean you understand your true
motivations and behavior patterns. If you understand your

inner drives, you are less apt to engage in denial and may be better able to see if your motivations will support or sabotage your business. Before you commit your resources and time to a new venture, it will be prudent to double check why you wish to start such a venture in the first place.

I remember a young person who, after being passed over for promotion, borrowed a few thousand dollars from his parents and bought the first business he could find. A year later he sold it for half the purchase price just to get out of it. As he came to understand later, his motivation was revenge against his boss, not the challenges and freedom of self-employment.

Match your talents with your goals
By being true to yourself you can match your talents with your goals. By contrast, a wishful image of yourself coupled with an unrealistic goal, in most instances, will result in failure.

Have you ever met anyone who thought they could make a lot of money in sales but lacked the aggressive personality necessary to close a deal? We see examples every day of people working at positions or professions for which they are ill-suited. And when they don't succeed, they don't understand why. Some are quick to blame others for their lack of success or happiness. Perhaps with a deeper understanding of themselves, their lives and their careers might have been more fulfilling. A business can be a task master to the owner. If the demands of the business don't match the talents of the owner, the chances of survival may be slim. Don't kid yourself, especially when it comes to your talents. Don't place yourself in a position that prevents you from dealing with the problems of business survival with objectivity and foresight. Deceptive thinking will cloud your judgment and lead to poor decisions. If you want to succeed, why bet against yourself?

Personality pitfalls and psychological danger signs

Let's take a look in greater detail at the major psychological reasons businesses fail. Being forewarned is being forearmed.

It's not my fault

Ask the person who has failed in business why the business failed and the probable answer will be the usual excuses ranging from not enough money to the unfair tactics of competitors. Customers and suppliers may be blamed as well. But as Shakespeare wrote, "Dear Brutus, the fault lies within us."

For a variety of reasons, a companion to failure is the denial of our part in it. In Atlanta, Georgia, Roger failed at developing a small mail order company, forcing him to return to his previous employer far poorer than when he left. Roger spent money recklessly on advertising and printed material with little consideration to the poor response he was generating. When he ran out of cash and closed his home-based company, Roger was quick to tell everyone that consumer pessimism did him in. He was convinced that in better economic times his little company would have succeeded. As Roger saw it, he was not to blame for his failure—the world was.

It's tough to say "I blew it"

As great an industrialist as Henry Ford was, he forgot to put a reverse gear in his first car. He corrected it and went on.

It's tough to say, "I blew it." The greatest mistake a person can make, however, is to deny any part in a failure. It is not easy to openly admit poor judgment, wishful thinking, impatience and even greed, but it's healthy and the first step to capitalizing on a failed business venture. There are many business owners who failed more than once and became successful by not denying their shortcomings. Just as an inflated ego can cause you to fail, the same ego can prevent you from learning from the unfortunate experience and trying again.

If you are reading this book after experiencing a business failure, study your mistakes and learn from them. Failure can be a very important part of success. Henry Ford felt that failure is the opportunity to begin again more intelligently.

Self-destruction
Some of us have a subconsciousness desire to create problems for ourselves. We set up and create situations that eventually lead to our self-destruction. This type of behavior, driven by hidden motives we may not understand, is deadly in business. It assures failure, unless we are very lucky.

It is a perplexing question why some people, after working diligently toward a cherished goal, somehow manage to "louse it up," avoiding the rewards of success. Consider the many tales of successful executives who, at some point in time, display inappropriate behavior such as philandering, gambling or excessive drinking—all actions of poor judgment. After a lifetime of hard work and proper judgment, they go "off the deep end," causing their own downfall. As psychologists tell us, certain types of personalities and traits can lead to self-destruction. Underlying the self-destruction path may be a "fear of success."

Procrastination

Do you know people who never seem to accomplish anything or people who have a myriad of excuses to postpone their responsibilities? They are procrastinators.

Procrastination is a personality problem that can place a business in jeopardy through neglect! It allows an owner to put off doing troublesome or unpleasant tasks. If a deposit hasn't been made, checks may bounce; or perhaps an insurance policy lapses because making a payment was delayed.

Procrastination is more than simple excuses such as, "I forgot," or "I have been too busy." It is defined by psychologists as deferring an important action until another day or time. It may be a mask for other more deep-rooted problems, which may also slow down the race for success. The problems of procrastination can show up in a number of ways that may not be easily recognizable, as discussed below.

Battle for control. Procrastination may also be a form of control over the actions of others. If someone is dependent on you to perform some task and you put it off, you may be sending a strong message of your own independence. Subconsciously, you may view cooperation as capitulation.

Procrastination allows you to deal with a situation on your terms, often to the detriment of the business. Business owners who make the statement "I'll get to it when I can" and then don't will soon alienate customers, employees and vendors. Unfortunately, their battle for control usually works against the business' chance for success because such a confrontational attitude discourages cooperation and teamwork. Overcontrol through procrastination is neglect that can kill a business venture.

Perfectionism. Fear of imperfection can be a form of delay. "If I can't do it perfectly, I won't attempt it at all" may be an excuse to cover up a fear of failing.

If you insist on perfection, you may be making excuses for your lack of action, which may function as a kind of insurance against failing. If you avoid some action, you can't be judged on your performance; or if you don't make a commitment or a decision, you are not responsible and can't be held accountable if things don't work out. A perfectionistic fear of failure may result in inaction or the inability to make decisions. Consequently, if you lack the courage to make a commitment to your business or the willingness to make a decision, it will be difficult for you to prosper. Putting off doing things can be safe until you pay the price of neglect.

Fear of success. The fear of success itself may also be a form of procrastination. A person may be just on the verge of realizing a dream when all of a sudden, without explanation, he or she quits. Many a new business has failed because the owner gave up too soon.

Psychologists say the fear of success is rooted in feelings of guilt and unworthiness. It seems as if the mere attainment of any degree of success creates an emotional conflict. The subconscious may appear to be yelling that you don't deserve your goal, attempting to undo your efforts to succeed.

The fear of success may be so strong that you constantly sabotage your efforts, leaving you wondering why you can't seem to succeed. Do you ever wonder why an individual who seems to have everything all of a sudden commits a foolish act or makes a stupid decision? It can be baffling to us as we wonder what goes on in a person's mind to invite such failure. Twelve-step, self-help groups abound with stories of personal experience ranging from actors who fail to keep important audition appointments to students who drop out of college during their last semester.

Such stories of individuals who manage to engineer failure have become the basis of many psychological studies of subconscious self-destruction. Have you not read about celebrities and politicians who have a difficult time dealing with their new status? It seems as if the successful person, upon reaching the peak, has a personality change. Sometimes, the diligent and hard-working individual becomes arrogant, careless, inconsiderate and may even profess invincibility.

How many entrepreneurs have caused their own failure? It is a question worth investigating by anyone about to jump into business. When we start out, some of us do so without regard to the consequences of failure to our family and friends. Our desire to grab a piece of the pie of success may be so strong that it clouds any concern of the possibility of failure. The fear of success is not easily recognizable and it has been my experience that it is an unusual person who will acknowledge it.

Being disorganized

Disorganization in a business can be disastrous. If you are the type of person who has difficulty in finishing anything or is easily distracted and always responds to the latest demand on your time, self-employment may not be for you. Being your own boss requires the self-discipline of structure and organization. Starting a million tasks and finishing but a few is wasteful of time and money.

Compulsiveness

Compulsive people can be risky in business. They may take action without thought or even concern for the present or future. If they wish to do something, regardless of the consequences, they do it. Compulsive individuals place their needs first, acting on impulse without thoughts of others. As a type, they exhibit poor judgment.

Can you be compulsive in business? Absolutely! For example, a compulsive entrepreneur may "feel" he or she must have a more prestigious location, better equipment, plush office space, a new car or first-class travel accommodations. The "must have" supersedes any rational analysis of a need that is emotionally driven.

Compulsively driven actions are disruptive to a business. Choices that owners and managers make are supposed to be for the ultimate good of the organization, not ego-enhancing pleasures or instant gratification for a single individual. When leading corporations search for a top executive, a major criteria for selection is a track record of good judgment and the ability to make the right decisions. It's tough to be compulsive and build a thriving business.

Lack of focus

Management books are full of comments about the value of setting goals and being objective. The very nature of business plans involve establishing specific objectives and laying out various marketing and financial plans to accomplish the desired goal. To succeed in business it's essential to remain focused on what it is you wish to accomplish. The lack of focus is a lack of direction. Successful ventures usually are well planned, with sets of contingencies to deal with unforeseen problems. Management must be focused to plan effectively.

To be focused means you must be able to zero in on your stated goal and do only those things that are important to the goal and not get sidetracked by unproductive distractions. I recall trying to work with an attorney who became so bogged down in meaningless side issues that it was impossible for him to complete my work. I was forced to seek other counsel.

I know of another situation where a business acquaintance began each day with a to-do list, but after the first hour in his office, the list was put aside to deal with more "pressing problems." He allowed himself to be too easily distracted. Many times, the problems were so minor that he wasted his time on trivia. To stay focused requires tough mental discipline, but it can be developed with practice and effort.

Lack of attention to detail

Contrary to the popular opinion of many success gurus, thinking big and avoiding detail can be a quick path to bankruptcy. Most failures are caused by the accumulation of small errors and waste. It is rare that a business goes under overnight due to some momentous event. Usually it is the gradual buildup of losses, uncollected customer balances, slow growth of inventory, unnoticed waste and rising expenses. Business owners who pay little attention to the details of their business are very apt to miss the developing trends of disaster.

Success means paying attention in close detail to what is going on in your business. It is important to delegate, but you can't delegate your responsibility for the welfare of your company. Paying attention to detail means knowing how much money your customers owe you, how much you owe your suppliers, how much money is in your checking account, how much dust is on your inventory and how accurate are your records.

Managers of larger companies rely on reports from others, whereas owners of smaller and newly-formed companies are in a position to observe firsthand what is going on. As a new firm grows, reports will replace the hands-on approach to management. Until such time, however, you should focus on the details of your daily transactions. And even when you do start receiving reports, closely examine and feel free to question the details of those reports.

My father was a successful business owner who believed that if you watched the pennies the dollars would take care of themselves. In my opinion, the only danger to detail is getting too enmeshed in it and losing sight of the dollars. Strive for balance, stay focused on your goals, but do not overlook the importance of detail. Overlooked errors and waste will result in losses and cash drain.

Lack of initiative
Some less-than-successful entrepreneurs are actually lazy. There are people who go into their own business because they do not want to work very hard. They believe, as an owner, they may issue orders, bark commands and wait for success. Employees are quick to discern just such a scenario. Lazy management will foster a less-than-enthusiastic work force.

I remember a situation where the owner of a modest manufacturing company who liked to party at night was always in conference every afternoon with his office couch. His office staff, aware of the situation, joked about it and took "long coffee breaks." He was eventually forced out of business by his more aggressive competitors. As most any small business operator will confirm, being on your own is hard work.

Immaturity

Immature leadership and management will drive out the best employees and keep the worst. Employees will quickly lose respect for owners who act immaturely and irrationally. It is unrealistic to expect your staff to be professional and exercise good judgment if you can't keep your emotions in check and be a leader. An owner's erratic emotions and mood swings are difficult for others to deal with. Such behavior undermines the sense of security and well being of employees and others. It also creates confusion and makes teamwork nearly impossible.

Greed and envy

What happens to greedy people? Their insatiable craving for more eventually distorts their sense of reality, fair play and even the reason they are in business. Greedy people do not function well in a team environment. Cooperation is not a comfortable place for the greedy as it involves trust and giving. If greed rules an entrepreneur, lasting relationships with suppliers and employees will be difficult to maintain. A fair business deal is where all parties benefit, not just the most demanding.

A new business needs help to survive; without it, the chances of success are even less than the already tough odds for survival. You can't expect customers, suppliers and employees to be there for you if you are only concerned about your personal gain. Greed has been responsible for many a business collapse.

Envy can be just as debilitating as greed and can seriously impair your judgment. Regardless of how well you are doing, with envy, you will always be dissatisfied, as there will always be a bigger competitor or a more successful acquaintance. Wanting too much too soon leads to overexpansion and bigger bills. Envy, like impatience, is an emotion and it does not belong in business.

Remember:
1. Try to understand yourself.
2. Be honest with yourself above all.
3. Know your limitations. Know where your talents lie.
4. If you fail, accept the blame and responsibility.
5. Don't deny your mistakes—learn from them.
6. Watch out for any self-destructive tendencies you may have.
7. Procrastination may jeopardize your business.
8. Don't use perfection as an excuse to delay.
9. Don't let feelings of guilt or a fear of success prevent you from succeeding.
10. Stay organized.
11. Be careful of the temptation to overcontrol.
12. Stay focused on your goals.
13. Remember detail counts.
14. Lazy entrepreneurs go broke.
15. Check any compulsive urges.
16. Childish entrepreneurs also go broke.
17. Watch out for feelings of greed or envy.

Chapter 2
Are there secrets to success?

If you are looking for guidance on how to be a successful entrepreneur, visit your local bookstore and you will find more advice books than you can read in 10 years. You will see works on selling, leadership, applying the techniques of ancient warriors, calling on the mysticism of the Orient, self-help therapy and even using God to get what you want. Or drop by your local library and you will find dozens of self-improvement titles.

Even late night cable television will entertain you with success commercials. For thirty minutes to an hour you can witness countless stories of remarkable transformations from poverty to yachts and mansions, documented with large blownup copies of cancelled checks made out to the newly rich. There is no shortage of books and courses on real estate profits, stock market killings, little-effort fortunes in mail order businesses, how to work at home and even earning money with your computer.

Don't overlook the full-page ads in the success magazines, where the author, for a fee, is willing to share his or her secret of success. Do you wonder, as I do, that if the person is so successful, why the need to sell the "secret?"

Today, you can borrow or buy all the instructions and plans you will ever need on how to achieve instant fame and fortune. These merchants of prosperity will have you believing success is something you can affordably buy or is a well-guarded secret that a group of wealthy individuals have mastered and may be willing to share for a large fee. In other words, success "sells."

Is success advice valid?

How much of this success advice and course material is valid? Is it written and produced only to earn the author income and guru status? I believe this is true in most cases. As for this book, I am mainly interested in: (1) promoting your welfare and (2) balancing the success glitz and glamour gimmicks with solid, down-to-earth, realistic information you can really use to avoid failure and achieve success.

Can *any* individual be taught a set of principles that will result in accomplishment? Can you teach success? Can someone through study bring about lasting significant personality change and undergo a transformation from an average person with limited drives and ambitions and skills to a high-powered entrepreneur? I don't think so!

Do you have the right stuff?

It will be wise for you to determine (ideally before you plunk down your money into a new venture) whether you have the "right stuff" to succeed. If you do, you can learn the steps and effort it takes to build a successful business. This book is about both how to determine if your personality lends itself to success or failure and what it takes to avoid failure and be successful.

Edward Moldt, Director of the Pappajohn Entrepreneurial Center at the University of Iowa has found that the most suc-

cessful entrepreneurs seemed to share the following traits:
1. Self-confidence: the ability to overcome fear of failure and inspire confidence in customers, investors and associates
2. Persistence: remaining inwardly optimistic and not shattered by frequent turndowns
3. Resilience: the inner strength to return after suffering frequent defeats
4. Vision: the ability to see where the company should go and how it should get there
5. Independence: getting satisfaction from being responsible to oneself and not to superiors
6. Daring: the ability to evaluate risk and not to be afraid of it.

A significant number of new business failures can be traced directly to the fact that the business founders did not have these traits required for success. They did not inspire confidence in anyone, including themselves. They may have been easily upset by problems and may have had difficulty in maintaining any internal optimism. They probably didn't develop a clear vision or realistic goal; instead they may have relied on wishful thinking.

Successful entrepreneurs consider the odds
Many of us at different moments in our lives have considered the idea of venturing out on our own but failure and risk must be analyzed first. There is no virtue in careless and clumsy stabs at going into business.

No new business is risk free. All start up ventures pose risk. Furthermore, the element of risk goes beyond the entrepreneur: it extends to creditors, landlords, employees and all parties connected to the venture. A business failure, no matter how small, touches many lives.

If you believe in fairy tales, then all entrepreneurs are winners.

However, pick up any book on entrepreneurs and you will find little coverage of risk or the price of failure—it is minimized. Successful entrepreneurs understand the element of risk. Only if the odds are in the favor of success in a given situation do they commit their capital. They certainly do not approach starting a business and risking their capital with an attitude of let's see what happens. Successful entrepreneurs are only one part dreamer and three parts realist.

Before starting any venture, it helps to understand the rules of successful entrepreneurship if you hope to beat the odds. Remember, successful entrepreneurs don't gamble; they invest in calculated risks. The odds of success and failure are carefully studied before cash is committed. Being a success in business is not a crap shoot! This is especially important information for a beginning entrepreneur who usually has little money to place at risk, leaving little margin for error.

Intelligent and objective planning and analysis come first. Wishful thinking has no place in the launching of a new business. Cautious thinking is important. As there are warning signs on highways to alert motorists to danger, businesses have their own language that seasoned entrepreneurs quickly recognize to help them avoid failure. In this book, I'll point out the signposts of danger.

Success: A few thoughts

1. Be cautious of "instant success" advice.

2. Be wary of all "secrets to wealth" offers. Remember it's probably the seller of secrets who will get rich, not you.
3. Be aware of what you risk before you start.
4. Remember, successful entrepreneurs don't gamble; they take calculated risks and they know the odds.

PART TWO
Mastering money

I find it strange that potential entrepreneurs who have difficulty balancing their household checkbook or managing their personal finances believe they can manage a business. If they lack an understanding of the fundamentals of money management, they will soon discover that their ability to survive in business will require more than simple recordkeeping. They will quickly become aware that their business success will demand that they have a knowledge of basic business finance. They will also need the discipline to efficiently work with limited funds and to be able to manage cash flow.

You can fail in business if you have too much money; you may fail if you do not know you are losing money; you will fail if you run out of money. These are all conditions or situations successful owners recognize and correctly deal with to avoid bankruptcy.

Chapter 3
Why having too much money is dangerous

Too much money may seem like a strange topic in a book on avoiding the pitfalls of starting a business, but having more money than you need to establish your venture can lead to your business's failure. Too much money may give you a false sense of security so you do not feel an urgent need to make your business profitable. Too much money will allow you to spend imprudently. Just what is "too much money?" It is when you have the luxury of waste.

Too much money clouds any sense of urgency or the immediate need to become quickly profitable. With the extra dollars in a checking account, an owner feels little pressure to work weekends or to make the usual sacrifices necessary for success. Unrealistically, a too-rich new entrepreneur can enjoy the fruits of success right from the start. Or so he or she thinks!

Too much money permits and encourages hasty expansion and unnecessary expenses, a common cause of business failure. If the money is available, an owner may be tempted to add staff, add facilities, expand product offerings, incur unwise promotional expenses, offer customers generous credit terms and even spend on lavish customer entertainment. The expansion of any business is easy, but contraction or "downsizing" is difficult and painful to owners and employees alike.

Even well-established companies with too much surplus cash have been known to become arrogant and indifferent to their customers—losing market share and even eventually declaring bankruptcy. These companies lost their sense of purpose and the need to satisfy their customers.

Roger's money

Roger, a young executive employed by a large chain of paint stores, had for some time wished to own a business. After inheriting a substantial sum of money, he left his employer, sold his home and moved to Florida to open his dream business: a painting equipment distributorship.

Roger wanted the best of everything for his new company. One of his first acts was to sign a five-year lease for a new building in an upscale industrial park. Next, he proceeded to design luxury offices, install new furnishings and fixtures and lease office equipment. To provide repair and warranty services for his customers, he outfitted a complete shop with the best of tools and equipment. He arranged with various manufacturers to become a distributor of equipment and repair parts. He invested heavily in inventory. His experience with his former employer strengthened his desire to be all things to all customers.

Roger then hired his father-in-law, who was unemployed at the time, as a salesperson, his wife (now his ex-wife) as the office manager and two local young persons to work in the store and shop. He found a nearby attorney and accountant. Everything was now in place. All he needed was customers.

To promote his company, he printed brochures, catalogs, business cards and assorted advertising materials. Slowly, the business began to develop.

Roger was aggressive in soliciting business. He and his father-in-law believed in cutting the price to make a sale, and if necessary, they offered generous credit terms to close the deal. The philosophy of the company was simple: Make the sale and worry about the profits later. Roger was determined his company was going to be an important distributor. His role model was a large competing distributor that appeared to have plenty of money and inventory. This competitor maintained a very aggressive posture—their goal was to dominate their market. Roger was convinced he could compete.

After a few months in business, Roger started to experience cash flow problems. His slow-paying customers, his inflated inventory and his excessive expenses all contributed to a significant cash shortage. Rather than run the risk of alienating a past due customer or cutting back on expenses, Roger bailed out his company with more money from his inheritance. As long as Roger had the money available, he was able to sustain a successful image and keep his company alive. It was easier to go to the bank and transfer funds from his personal account to his business account than to make tough decisions. His money allowed him to postpone dealing with his problems.

The day the money ran out, Roger's life became a nightmare. He was unable to pay his bills. His wife had little tolerance for frugality and filed for divorce. His father-in-law quit. And his vendors were threatening to sue. Roger was broke and in debt. He was forced to sell part of his company to keep it going.

Lack of urgency

If you have more money or credit than you need, it may lead you to inept money management, waste and unnecessary expense. As most new businesses will lose money for at least the first year, it may deplete the owner's investment as the cash is drained from the company. A sense of false security from initially having too much cash on hand or available credit removes any sense of urgency to work quickly at stopping losses before the money runs out. After the initial investment is gone, only new investment or debt will keep the firm alive.

If you are leaving the secure confines of corporate America, leave some of your work habits behind. With your new venture, you must develop a sense of urgency—you must take action! If you are accustomed to spending long hours in committee meetings deliberating a project or problem, this is a luxury that your new business, fighting to survive, can ill afford. While it is wise to seek other opinions, committees cost money and waste time. Too much money will permit a bloated management structure that is not efficient in any organization and deadly for your new firm. If you hire a staff just to hold meetings to agree with your decisions, you may be charting a strategy of failure.

Frank did. He left a Fortune 500 company after 23 years to establish a small advertising agency. Frank is a talented graphic designer with a very pragmatic approach to life but without a sense of urgency. Unfortunately, his small agency closed its doors after thirteen months of operation because he ran out of money. He believed he was doing everything right. He spent a great deal of time developing a very detailed business plan. He and his two employees conducted daily staff meetings to assure communication and morale. Everything ran smoothly; the only problem was the lack of clients. Frank did not understand the need to develop and obtain customers quickly. He was used to "corporate life" with its emphasis on planning and meetings. Frank found it difficult to adjust to a sense of urgency to survive. He never understood "what is the rush?" He returned to his former employer, a disappointed person.

Expansion

A common theme in management is the perceived need to grow, to expand and to outpace your competitor. This idea of "bigger is better" is so ingrained in the psyche of American business that most anyone starting a business wants to grow quickly. However, such over- and premature expansion are common causes of business failure. If you have the money, you may be tempted to expand but if you do not have it, you simply cannot expand.

Too rapid an expansion will result in losses and a cash drain. It is a gamble of more immediate expenses in anticipation of rising income. From it, you may expect a negative cash flow depleting your reserves as your expenses, such as payroll, insurance and overhead, grow faster than your sales income.

Beyond that, there is the danger you may lose control. Too rapid an expansion creates control problems. Your existing financial and operational systems may not be adequate to handle your new employees, customers and products. Your company will "strain at the seams." If your business spins out of control, it will be inefficient and mistake prone. Unless corrected, it will self-destruct through losses and debt.

Excess inventory

When you start out, be careful that too much money doesn't

quickly turn into too much inventory. You will find suppliers eager to sell to you and they may even pressure you to buy more than you need. Just because you may have the money to invest, don't be like some entrepreneurs who are so concerned about missing a sale, they try to stock everything they think their customers will ever ask for.

As a case in point, I recall considering the purchase of a distributor of fasteners (nuts, bolts, rivets and clamps). I quickly became aware that the company was suffering financially because most of the company funds were tied up in large amounts of slow- and nonmoving inventory. During my onsite visit I inspected the warehouse, and as I walked up and down the aisles between the storage racks, I noted a substantial inventory, most of it very dusty. Inventory that does not sell collects dust—a bad sign.

Later in the owner's office, as we talked about his company, I asked about the inventory control system and what procedures he used to order merchandise. The owner told me that there was no need to spend time and effort on any expensive inventory control system as he could "eyeball" what he needed to order. He also pointed out that he prided himself on rarely being out of stock on any product a customer ordered.

As the company maintained over 5,000 different sized fasteners, I will never forget his comment of "eyeballing" his inventory. As far as I know, he did not sell the company and continues to increase his inventory through mismanagement.

Generous credit terms
Some foolish entrepreneurs, more hungry for customers than

money, use liberal credit terms as an incentive to persuade potential customers to buy. Their use of such liberal credit terms rapidly transforms their money into slow-paying or uncollectible accounts receivable.

If you have plenty of available cash, you may be tempted to be generous with your credit terms to get your customers' business. After all, if you need cash, it's easy to use your reserves or your credit line to finance your bills. Entrepreneurs who are careless about offering credit to customers are flirting with bankruptcy. To avoid losing your money with deadbeats or scam artists, you should follow these basic principles of effective credit management: conduct credit checks on all new customers; watch your credit terms; establish collection procedures; and don't wait too long to aggressively collect from customers. Remember, it's your money at risk!

Starting out, you may be so eager to sell your products or services that you mistakenly assume any potential customer's credit is good. Victor did. During his first year of business, while operating a small distributorship of recording accessories, he extended credit without question to any retail store that ordered from him. Unfortunately, almost a third of his customers ended up being "deadbeats." As it turned out, he was the only supplier that would give them credit. Victor lost much money and his distributorship almost failed.

In another situation, the owner of a new distributor of audio products eagerly accepted a large order after being told by the sales representative that the customer urgently needed the product. The day the shipment arrived at the customer's store, the sheriff locked the front door in bankruptcy proceedings.

Unfortunately, the distributor could not get the product back. Two years later the distributor received a token settlement—what a costly mistake!

A frequent cause of new business failure results from extending credit to customers who do not pay their bills. You need to keep a close watch over your customers' balances if you intend to be paid. You need a system (which you'll read about in the next chapter) that will alert you to collection problems. After all, it is your money they are holding.

As I have noted, cash or credit reserves that are not necessary can become a crutch that permits the unwise entrepreneur to avoid facing the reality that the business is headed for trouble. Such easy access to additional money during the critical first year will lessen the need to act quickly and prudently to get the firm on a solid footing. Instead, as you put together your financing to launch your dream, you should plan carefully to determine the minimum (not the maximum) amount of money you will need to run your business. Do not borrow or invest more than that amount, as too much money removes any sense of urgency, encourages premature expansion and encourages unnecessary spending.

Remember:
1. Watch your spending, especially if you can afford it.
2. Avoid premature expansion.
3. Have a sense of urgency.
4. Rush to get profitable and stop the losses.
5. Avoid committees and time-wasting meetings.
6. Know if you are profitable or not.
7. Avoid excess inventory at all costs.

Chapter 4
Money:
You need it to survive

Money, in my opinion, is the most important asset of a start-up business. Without it, a business will slide into financial difficulty or failure. The lack of cash reserves is a serious matter. You may have invested a great deal of your resources and yourself into your business, but if you fail to manage your cash flow, you may be forced out of business. You can make mistakes in managing your employees, your customers or your physical facilities and your business will probably survive. But if you don't manage your cash, your company will become a business statistic.

In this chapter, I will show you how to become selfish with your cash. I will point out techniques you can use to speed up your collections and some strategies you can use to hoard your cash. In fact, some of the techniques I will be sharing with you were responsible for the survival of a business I am still active in.

What happens when your checkbook is empty?
Assume it's Friday morning. Your checking account is overdrawn and you must make out paychecks for your two employees. What do you do? How do you tell them they won't be getting paid today? If this is the first time, they probably will

not quit on you and may even be a little understanding. However, their families may not be so tolerant. If, on the following Friday, there is still no money, be prepared to look for new employees.

Or, it is Wednesday afternoon and the telephone company notifies you that unless they have a certified check by noon the next day, your phones will be shut off. When your suppliers and customers hear that your phones have been disconnected, they will be aware that your business is in trouble. It certainly will shake the confidence of those you need the most.

These are tough situations to be in, but as experienced and successful business owners have learned, cash planning is vital to prevent the difficult and embarrassing problems an empty checkbook will create. Any debt that is not paid will cause you problems, but nothing like not paying your employees, the telephone company, your landlord or your taxes.

Your employees
I watched a manufacturing company that I was doing business with create problems with their labor force because their payroll checks frequently bounced. The owners, struggling to keep the business alive, felt the employees should be more understanding of the tough times the company was experiencing. But when a machine operator earning just above the minimum wage receives a "rubber" paycheck about once a month and walks by the owner's Mercedes on the way to the employee parking lot, understanding is not likely to be there.

Your employees are an important part of your investment in your company. A highly-skilled labor force, well-versed in a firm's operations may be irreplaceable. To develop such a work force, you must recruit the best employees you can afford, you must train them and you must work to gain their loyalty and dedication to your company. All your efforts will be wasted if they don't get paid. If conditions are difficult and you have developed a relationship of trust and honesty with them, you probably can miss one payday, but not two or three.

Your utilities
You will find that you are as dependent upon the utility and telephone companies as you are upon your most important suppliers. If service is shut off, your company may be shut down. Try to operate any business without electricity. If your office is dark and computers are off, you are, in effect, closed!

I knew of an insurance broker, deep in debt due to gambling, who stole electricity. He operated a small insurance agency located near New York City. Because he could not pay his bill and dared not be without electricity, he managed to get into the basement area of the building and tap into his neighbor's electrical junction box. He stole electricity for almost two years. He lost his insurance license and almost went to jail.

How you become poor from poor cash management
Helen, who owned a small commercial art studio, worked 12-hour days, Monday through Saturday to meet her customers' demands. Although she had only two employees and minimal expenses, she was rarely able to draw a paycheck for herself. Fortunately, her spouse earned a substantial salary, permitting Helen to continue working without bringing home any money.

She had absolutely no idea about cash management. She

struggled to pay her employees, her landlord and her vendors. To make matters worse, she had fallen behind in depositing payroll taxes and the IRS placed a lien on her husband's retirement real estate in the Southwest. She could not even turn to her accountant for assistance as she had owed him money for two years. Helen did not understand it. Her customers loved her. She was always busy. But she was always broke.

Helen lacked organizational skills. Her financial records were a mess. Her customers owed her thousands of dollars that she never attempted to collect. Plus, she was never quite sure of the amount anyone owed her as she frequently forgot to prepare customer bills or enter them into her accounts receivable ledger.

Unfortunately, Helen was an easy prey for unscrupulous people. She was overly generous to all and sympathized with her customers when they explained why they could not pay her. Helen even acted as a surrogate mother to some, listening to their tales of woe and allowing emotion to get in the way of good business practices. She rarely asked them for her money. There was a particular customer who owed her $3,000 for over three years and never attempted to pay her. Yet, she continued to do work for this customer, spending her own money on supplies and labor to do the customer's jobs. Someone sarcastically said to her that she might as well do the work for free and save herself the trouble of bookkeeping.

Finally, after much pressure from her spouse, she was willing to listen and accept advice on the principles of cash management. She hired a part-time small business consultant to help her revamp and upgrade her accounting system by installing a personal computer. Once the records were correct, the consultant called a number of customers to collect money. The situation improved, but barely, as many of the past-due customers turned out to be dishonest with no intention of paying her. It did not take long for Helen's old habits of mismanagement, disorganization and foolish generosity to return. The consultant quit and eventually the business failed.

Helen's failure is an example of avoiding or not wanting to learn the basics of simple cash management. Helen created her own problems as her main interest was in being creative, not managing her business.

Forecast your cash needs monthly

Don't wait for a problem to develop: anticipate it! If your checking account is bumping along just above zero and cash flow problems are a way of life, forecasting your cash requirements and cash availability is vital to your business's survival. Here is a simple, but effective, method that I have used. It works as a temporary measure, gaining you time to find solutions to your problems.

Assume it is the beginning of the month, your checking account balance is low as usual and you are facing your customary cash demands. Before doing anything else, first prepare a list of the overhead expenses you must meet—that is, your wages, rent, utility bills, installment debt or any mandatory monthly payments. These obligations are your first priority bills—obligations you must pay, to keep the doors open and your employees with you. Next, prepare a list of bills from your suppliers and vendors for such items as inventory and supplies. This list represents your second priority obligations, which can be flexible, unlike your first list.

After you have completed the two lists, prepare an estimate of the amount of cash you can expect from your accounts receivable collections and cash sales, if any, during the coming month. If you have been in business for a while, review the last few months' cash receipts as a guide to your forecast. Keep it realistic, no wishful thinking. Good cash management demands realistic expectations.

Make simple cash analysis work for you—especially in a crisis
To illustrate, I have prepared an example (Table 1) of a simple cash analysis report. First, start with the checking account balance at the beginning of the month, which in this example is $1,000. Next add estimated collections and any other cash receipts ($23,000) giving a total of $24,000 available to pay all of the bills and obligations.

If the first priority bills total $11,000 and the second priority bills total $18,000, a strategy to deal with a cash shortage is needed.

If the cash receipts forecast is accurate, after paying the first priority expenses such as wages and taxes, there will be a balance of only $13,000 left to pay second priority bills (such as suppliers). There is going to be a cash shortage of $5,000 since total bills and obligations are $29,000.

Table 1
A Simple Cash Analysis Report

ITEM	AMOUNT ($)
Beginning checking account balance	$ 1,000
Estimated collections	$23,000
Estimated cash available for the current month	$24,000

Less: total cash requirements for
 the current month $29,000

Consisting of Priority 1 and Priority 2 expenses:
 Priority 1 expenses:

Wages	$ 5,000
Payroll and sales taxes	$ 2,000
Utilities	$ 1,000
Leases	$ 3,000
Total Priority 1 expenses =	$11,000

Cash available for priority 2 expenses:
 $24,000 estimated cash available less
 $11,000 Priority 1 expenses = $13,000

Priority 2 expenses:

XYZ Supply Company	$ 7,000
ABC Manufacturing	$ 6,000
Misc. suppliers	$ 5,000
Total Priority 2 expenses =	$18,000

Estimated shortage ($24,000 cash less $11,000 Priority 1 expenses less $18,000 Priority 2 expenses) = ($5,000)

This is a cash-flow crisis—available cash of $24,000 is less than the $29,000 needed to pay all the bills. Nevertheless, there are some available options. Suppliers can be flexible creditors, as it usually is in their best interest not to push their customers into bankruptcy. Don't misunderstand me; debts must be paid.

However most suppliers will "work" with their customers and allow a flexible payment schedule as a temporary solution. The most effective approach is to call each supplier, explaining that the present cash flow is slow but that as much cash as possible will be sent as soon as possible. It is always advantageous to take the initiative. Don't wait until the suppliers call you—they may not be as cooperative.

Emergency Savings Account. Continuing with this example, I would suggest putting $2,000 of the $13,000 earmarked for our suppliers in a special emergency savings account and send each supplier the following amounts:

Table 2
Payment Schedule

SUPPLIER	AMOUNT DUE	AMOUNT PAID
XYZ Supply company	$ 7,000	$ 5,000
ABC Manufacturing	$ 6,000	$ 3,500
Misc. suppliers	$ 5,000	$ 2,500
TOTAL	$18,000	$11,000

With this approach the cash problem has been managed by sending each supplier one-half or more of what is owed and "bought" precious time—time to aggressively seek ways to improve the cash flow. As suppliers will eventually insist on payment in full, this approach is a temporary solution.

To be able to stay in business, a continuing cash shortage will force an owner to change the way business is done. Among the needed changes may be reducing expenses, tightening credit terms to customers, increasing sales or increasing prices.

You must accept the fact you will always have bills. Regardless of how much you are struggling with a daily problem of not having enough cash, put a small percentage of each deposit in the emergency savings account. If you save just five cents of each dollar you collect, in 20 months you will have saved an amount equal to a month's collections. And, before you disregard my advice as impractical, remember, if you squirrel away some money and delay paying some of your bills, you still have the money and can pay the bill(s) earlier if you so decide. Try saving the five percent of collections—it will make a difference to your business's survival.

Let me conclude with an example of a cash-reserve strategy I have seen used successfully. Assume you are a small distributor of auto parts and you sell a piece of equipment that cost you $2,000 for $3,000 to a local gas station. Your supplier extends 90-day terms to you, but you only extend credit terms of 30 days. A month from the date of the sale the customer pays you the $3,000. You deposit the cost of the equipment ($2,000) in the emergency savings account and the $1,000 balance in the checking account. Sixty days later you withdraw the $2,000 from the savings account and pay your supplier. Holding onto the money for the 60 days allows you to earn interest on the money and increase the cash position of your balance sheet. As you have the money, you can always pay the bill. If your cash flow improves over the next two months, you probably can pay the bill without withdrawing the $2,000 from your savings account. Thus, you have built a cash reserve without going to the bank for a loan. You have created an emergency fund by learning how to work with other people's money.

Two other essential savings accounts

Earlier in this chapter, I wrote about establishing a special emergency savings account. If you are having cash shortages and living on the edge as you struggle to establish your business, two additional small savings accounts are a vital part of your survival strategy. You should open separate accounts for payroll tax and for sales tax.

An easy way to get into financial trouble is by not depositing the payroll taxes that you deduct from your employees' paychecks. It is very tempting to pay only the net amount of the paychecks and plan to pay the taxes later when you have the money. After all, you have other bills to pay and the taxes may not due be yet. But watch out: if you postpone the payroll taxes too long, you will have a whopping bill with penalties and interest added on. A simple way to avoid the problem is to immediately deposit the amount of the tax deductions in a payroll savings account and pay the taxes due on time before you use the money to pay some other bills.

I assume you are aware of the advice financial planners give about paying yourself first as a way of building savings. The same excellent advice applies to any small business having tough times staying afloat.

Also open a separate account for sales taxes. While, it may not seem like much at the time of sale, the accumulation of sales taxes by the end of the tax reporting period can be significant. Keep your sales tax collections in a special sales tax savings account and you will avoid an unnecessary problem.

Establish effective collection procedures

When I taught entrepreneurship and began to discuss collections and credit, I would usually start the discussion by asking if anyone had lent money to a friend and was reluctant to ask for it. In response, I heard comments about hating to ask for things and wishing to avoid unpleasant situations. My experience has shown me if you cannot ask for your money, you should not be in business. If you do dislike asking for money, get over it; get used to chasing your customers to get paid. The cliché "a squeaky wheel gets the grease" is appropriate for managing your receivables. Don't assume any of your customers will pay you on time. If it is in your best interest to hold onto your cash as long as possible, it is also in their best interest to do likewise. The phrase "ask and you shall receive" is the motto of any experienced credit manager.

You must protect your money. Require all new customers wishing credit to submit references. Be suspicious if a new customer insists on immediate credit. Also, be cautious of glowing reports from unknown references—they may actually be relatives of the applicant posing as credit references. If you do receive reports of slow payment, be careful!

First of all, if you extend credit to a customer, give or send a bill immediately. I recently had some electrical work done on my home and had to call the contractor three times to obtain a bill. I wonder how many bills he forgot to send out and how many customers "forgot" to call him? Establish a firm policy that no service is to be performed or any merchandise shipped without an accompanying invoice. Remember, in the situation of Helen and her ad agency she loved doing the jobs, but she hated the paperwork. Her customers never complained that she neglected to bill them and yours won't either.

In fact, many customers may find it helpful to receive two copies of your invoice, one they keep for their records and a duplicate one to be sent back to you with the check. Receiving a copy of the invoice with a customer's check helps your book-keeping by identifying the correct invoice, particularly important if you have sent several different invoices to a customer for different work or services. Sending a self-addressed, stamped return envelope can speed up payment, too.

Besides the invoices, it is important to send monthly statements listing your customers' payments and all unpaid invoices. Some of your customers may not keep accurate records or lose or forget to record your invoices. A statement tells your customers you are well aware of what is owed to you and you expect payment. Businesses that don't send statements are sending a message that invites exploitation by unscrupulous customers. The effects of statements are well worth the time and postage.

In one New York town, there was a distributor of swimming pool supplies that refused to send statements to customers because, in the opinion of the owner, "It is the responsibility of the customers to keep track of their bills." He felt it was sufficient to issue an invoice at the time of sale. Unfortunately, the customers did not keep track of their bills and he eventually was forced into bankruptcy when his cash flow trickled to near nothing. When it comes to collecting money, it does not pay to stand on principle. It can be self-defeating.

It is never enough to insure a good cash flow by just sending invoices and statements. You must aggressively manage your receivables, the money owed to you. Vital to any successful collection activity is an accurate and current payment history of each customer. You must establish a method to monitor your accounts receivables. The usual system is to list all your customers with all of their unpaid invoices grouped by the number of days past due. Accountants refer to this process as "aging accounts receivable." Most all small business accounting software programs contain such aging reports. You need to know who owes you money, how much they owe you and how long they have owed it to you!

Here are some collection techniques that are very effective and should not offend your customers:

1. As soon as payment is past due, send a copy of the invoice to the customer with a notation requesting their check.
2. When you send out a monthly statement, circle the past due invoices.
3. A handwritten note on a statement or invoice is more effective than computer-printed messages or past-due stamps and stickers. It alerts the customer that you are aware of the delinquent account.
4. Sometimes a phone call to the customer asking when you may expect a check can work.
5. Telling your customer that you have some large bills coming due and that you would appreciate a little help with a check can be effective if not used too often.

If none of these tactics work, you need to employ more aggressive ones. You may lose the customer, but remember the older the bill, the less chance you have of ever seeing the money. Bank loan officers and other credit managers are well aware of the problem of past-due debt. They know that the older the debt, the less the possibility of collecting it.

Attorney Robert Dickinson said, "Bad debts are not like good wine—they don't get better with age."

Here are five very aggressive collections strategies:
1. Telephone the customer demanding a check and threaten to turn the account over to a collection agency.
2. If the customer claims to have no money now, ask for a post-dated check.
3. If possible, a very effective approach is to pay a visit to the customer and demand a check on the spot.
4. Consistent and frequent follow-up calls will usually get your money unless you are dealing with an unscrupulous and dishonest individual.
5. Have your attorney send a letter demanding payment or you will begin legal action. This can be very effective.

Collection agencies
I have never had much success with collection agencies. It has been my experience they don't believe in wasting time chasing deadbeats. If you turn over a list of delinquent accounts to the average agency, they will try to collect the easy ones and forget the rest! Besides, collection agencies are expensive. You may pay them as much as 40 percent of the amount collected. Not very profitable!

I recommend you use an agency only when you have made every effort to collect the funds, nothing has worked and you are about to write off the amount to bad debt. Certainly you should never engage the services of a collection firm merely because you don't like to make calls asking for money.

You can always sue
If there are large amounts owed to you, consider hiring an attorney. Habitual slow payers are experienced with thwarting the efforts of collection agencies but may fear legal action.

Some of us are quick to call a lawyer to settle our affairs. But lawsuits are slow and expensive. Here is an example of what can happen when you extend credit to the wrong customer and you use an attorney to sue.

Assume a customer owes you $10,000 and ignores all of your attempts to collect. Your calls are never returned, your notes go unacknowledged and even your attorney's letters go unanswered. Finally, with no alternative, you proceed to sue. Here are some possible outcomes:
1. Your attorney draws up papers and arranges for a summons to be delivered to your customer.
2. The summons allows your customer time to respond to the suit to prepare a defense.
3. If your customer does not intend to pay you, the customer may begin a countersuit claiming defective product or fraud on your part creating a delaying tactic.
4. The case will be scheduled for a future court date according to the court's schedule.
5. Just before the actual court appearance, your customer may be willing to settle for half the amount and drop the

countersuit.
6. Your attorney will probably advise you to accept the offer as there is no guarantee of your doing any better before the judge.
7. You accept. Your attorney obtains a check from the defendant for $5,000, keeps at least half and forwards a check to you for $2,500. You won!

Or did you? Unfortunately, your victory cost you $7,500 and untold amounts of aggravation and emotional distress. You extended credit to a customer and after months of trying to collect, you are forced to sue. The lawsuit went on for months or longer and you wound up with only $2,500. I would say your customer won by paying only 50 percent of the amount owed to you.

Even if you win a judgment against a debtor, you only have a piece of paper that says you are entitled to collect the cash due to you. Your attorney may have to file for disclosure of the debtor's assets or arrange for the sheriff to auction assets to raise the money to pay you.

To make matters even worse, some clever deadbeats are judgment-proof. That means you can't collect even if you win your case in court. They manage to transfer or hide ownership of their assets in case someone wins a lawsuit and obtains a judgment against them.

Avoid the problem
It pays to avoid the problem in the first place. Would you lend $1,000 to a stranger for 30 days? I doubt it. If you treat giving credit to new customers the same as lending money, you will

become cautious when extending credit. To protect yourself you must check credit references. There are commercial services that will provide you information such as Dunn & Bradstreet. However, such information may not always be reliable. Your best bet is to check with other firms who are doing business with the potential customer. Call the credit managers of such firms and ask for a frank opinion. It pays—and saves you grief and losses.

Remember:

As I wrote in the first line of this chapter, money is the most important asset a start-up business has! Your business can not survive without it.

Whatever you do, don't run out of money because if you do:
1. Your employees will quit.
2. The telephone company will disconnect you.
3. You may be tempted to commit a desperate act.

To have money you must:
1. Check credit references.
2. Be aggressive about collecting money.
3. Forecast your cash needs and collections.
4. Forget about relying on collection agencies to collect your money.
5. Be able to collect money without relying upon suing.
6. Pay your bills wisely, remembering your first and secondary priorities.
7. If cash is short, stretch your payments by first calling creditors and then sending small amounts, if possible.
8. Establish separate savings accounts for taxes and emergencies.

Chapter 5
Are you making money?

John, the owner of a small landscaping supply company, left it up to his accountant to tell him if he was making money. John loved sales and promotion but financial details bored him. Finally, after months of losses, he ran out of cash. Alarmed with the possibility of failure, he began to pay attention to the finances of his company before it was too late. His business barely survived.

Supposedly, surviving in business is easy—just earn a consistent profit that converts to cash. That sounds simple but how do you know if your business is profitable? Ask yourself these three questions and if all the answers are yes, your business is probably profitable:

1. Is your business worth more this month than last month?
2. Are your cash balances increasing?
3. Are you able to pay your bills on time?

In this chapter I will first show one simple way to help you determine quickly whether your company is making or losing money: the equity report. This report is a time-tested survival tool you will find invaluable. Then, you'll see five power financial tools that can make or break your business: inventory turnover, accounts receivable rate of turnover, gross profit (margin) ratio, budgets and break-even analysis.

In the Appendix, I also explain how to use two financial documents that are mandatory if you want to stay in business and be successful: the balance sheet and the income statement. It's essential to read the Appendix to understand how these two financial statements are created and the role they play in helping you manage your business. (See pages 287 to 293.)

The Equity Report: The one-page financial statement to see if you're profitable

I will never forget a conversation over lunch one day with my close friend Murray, a successful distributor of shipping materials. During our chat, Murray told me that he didn't care about accounting and financial statements—all he wanted to know each month was how much cash he had, how much inventory he had on hand, how much was owed to him and how much he owed. If his inventory and the amount that was owed to him was larger than his bills, he had made money. Simple!

What Murray was talking about is a simplified accounting system (known as a "current equity report") that a New York merchant had taught him when he first started out in business. This simple system told Murray if he had made or lost money each month.

This is how it works. At the end of each month, he would add what was owed to him (his accounts receivable), his inventory and cash and then subtract what he owed (his accounts payable). The result of this addition and subtraction was his "equity." If the equity at the end of the current month increased over the prior month he had made a profit. A decrease meant he lost money. If you study the example in Table 3, you will see how Murray's system worked. From month one to month two, the total of cash, accounts receivable and inventory increased by $6,000, whereas the liabilities (debts) increased by $1,000. The net result was a gain in equity of $5,000—or in other words, a profit.

Table 3
Murray's Equity Report: An Example

ITEM	MAY ($)	JUNE ($)	DIFFERENCE ($)
Cash	3,000	2,000	
Accounts Receivable	16,000	22,000	
Inventory	19,000	20,000	
TOTAL	38,000	44,000	+6,000
Accounts Payable	28,000	29,000	+1,000
Equity	10,000	15,000	+5,000

In my courses on entrepreneurship, I stress this approach to those who do not have a background in accounting as a means of quickly determining profitability. (For those of you knowledgeable about accounting, you can see that I have taken a liberty with the term "equity," as I have purposefully omitted anything beyond current assets and liabilities.)

The report is easy to prepare and should be done at the end or beginning of every month. Whichever time period you elect (for example, the first or the last day of the month), be consistent.

First, add up your business bank accounts including all your checking and savings accounts. With that task completed, total the amount your customers owe you (every month you must prepare a list of customers and the balances owed to you).

Now, prepare a total dollar value of your inventory (using what you would get if all the inventory were sold). If you do not have inventory records, now is the time to prepare them.

Add up those three items: your cash, your customers' balances and the value of your inventory. These are the items on the plus side. From this total, you'll subtract all your bills from suppliers, operating expenses (such as utilities, rent as well as other items such as taxes) and other monthly payments you must make. The difference is your equity. It is the amount of cash on hand after selling all of your inventory, collecting all the monies owed to you by your customers and paying your current bills in full.

Remember, if the amount of your equity is increasing, you are earning a profit. (Let your accountant worry about the taxes and you worry about your business surviving.) The purpose of the "equity report" is not to replace your traditional financial statements (discussed in the Appendix), but to give you a simplified shortcut to make sure you are immediately aware of your profits or losses of the prior month.

Inventory turnover

As you know, inventory is an investment that ties up your cash resources until the inventory is sold and the amount owed is collected. You can increase your available cash by learning about "inventory turnover."

Imagine you buy and then resell 100,000 units of a product each year. Inventory turnover is the number of units of inventory divided by the cost of the units. For example, if you make one purchase of 100,000 units of inventory at the beginning of the year for $100,000, your inventory turnover per year will be (1) one. You are tying up $100,000 of your money for up to a year.

If instead, you buy in increments of 10,000 units ten times per year, you are keeping your inventory to a minimum by buying frequently. Now your turnover rate is 10 (100,000 units divided each $10,000 purchase). Your average investment in inventory will only be $10,000 and you'll free up quite a bit of your cash. A start-up business needs every available dollar.

The "80/20" principle will help you to maximize your inventory turnover. Mass merchandisers have long known that of the items in their inventory, only 20 percent of these items generate approximately 80 percent of dollar sales. And the 80 percent of slower-selling inventory items generates only 20 percent of dollar sales.

If only a small number of the inventory selections generate the bulk of the sales, then the majority of inventory selections tie up money in slow-moving merchandise.

Visit a major bookstore and you will discover the bulk of book sales are the best sellers. *The New York Times'* number one best-selling fiction title will probably sell 100 copies to the one copy of Charles Dickens's *Hard Times.* Where should you invest your inventory dollars? The 80/20 principle applies to any type of business that maintains significant inventories spread over a variety of different items from book titles to nuts and bolts.

If your objective is to maximize your turnover, you will focus on the twenty percent "best sellers" in your business.

When you shouldn't maximize inventory turnover
If you are trying to cultivate a loyal customer following by always having what your customers want, your inventory investment will be much larger—sacrificing turnover. Attempting to hold their customers with large and extensive inventories, various auto parts stores are always fighting the problem of too much dust-laden stock.

If you are starting a business that will be maintaining an inventory of many types of items or products, do this:
1. Maintain accurate inventory records.
2. Don't stock anything you don't sell at least one of every 60 days or 6 units per year: turnover of 6 times.
3. When a customer wants an item you do not stock, consider offering to special order it. You may find it is cheaper to arrange for overnight delivery from your supplier than to buy it for an occasional sale. Who knows when you will sell the next one? Take a lesson from the Japanese concept of "Just in Time."
4. Develop the inventory policy that is best for your business and your customers. For future planning, keep records of those items your customers want but you do not regularly stock.
5. Use the information to establish your inventory policy.

Accounts receivable rate of turnover

Your accounts receivables is your faith in your customers' credit-worthiness. Any supplier or bank from which you wish to have credit will want to know if your accounts receivables are solid—can your customers pay you and how long will they take to do so?

The best way to measure the creditworthiness of your customers is to compute your "accounts receivable rate of turnover." To calculate it, divide your annual gross sales by the total of your average accounts receivable.

For example, if your annual sales are $600,000 and the total of your customers' average balances is $100,000, then your accounts receivable turnover rate is 6 times per year ($600,000 divided by $100,000 equals 6) or the average customer balance is 2 months (12 months divided by 6, the accounts receivable ratio) or 60 days old. If your accounts receivable balances are $200,000 with the same sales amount of $600,000, your turnover will be 3 ($600,000 divided by $200,000 equals 3) or the average age of 120 days (360 days divided by 3).

The credit terms you offer your customers affect the accounts receivable rate of turnover. Major corporations can afford to be generous but you probably cannot. Try to offer payment terms of no longer than 30 days. If you can do it, try 10 days.

Gross profit (margin) ratio

Gross profit can be a confusing term. It is the profit left to pay your expenses with after you pay for the product you sold. To be more specific, if you buy a product for $1 and resell it for $2, your gross profit is $1. It is from this $1 that you must pay your expenses, such as rent and wages. Gross profit is traditionally measured as a percentage of sales and expressed as the gross profit margin or ratio, which is determined by the difference between the selling price and the product cost. Here's an example:

1. If you pay $1 for the item and sell it for $2, you will have a gross profit of 50 percent ($1 profit divided by $2 in sales) or $1. Any change in your selling price will change your margin. If you reduce your sales price by 50¢ to $1.50, your margin drops from $1 to 50¢ and is now 33% (50¢ divided by $1.50).
2. If you increase your original selling price by 50¢ to $2.50 the gross profit will jump to $1.50 or 60% .
3. On the other hand, any change in the price you pay for the product (your cost) will change your gross profit. If your supplier reduces your cost to 75¢ for the item and you continue to sell at $2, the gross profit will increase to $1.25 or a 25% increase. If you are forced to pay more for the product and cannot pass the increase along with higher selling prices, the gross profit will shrink, leaving less to cover over expenses.
4. Remember, the gross profit is always squeezed between the cost of the product and the selling price. A change in either affects it.

The business credit reporting firm Dunn and Bradstreet publishes gross profit ratios by type of business and industry. It is available in most libraries. It is helpful to compare your gross profit margin with other firms in your industry. As a rule, retail stores attempt to operate with gross profits of 40 to 50%, wholesalers at approximately 25 to 30% and manufacturing companies in the vicinity of 40%.

Budgets: Not just for the Fortune 500

A budget is difficult—difficult to put together and difficult to follow but a necessity for a new business if it is going to survive. A budget is a vital and important management and planning tool and should not be used just as a limit on spending.

A budget is a projected income statement. Income is estimated and projected over the forthcoming fiscal (company) year. Expenses are treated the same. From these projections the actual budget is developed. There are many computer software programs that will assist you in putting your budget together. Most accounting programs contain a section on budgets that will take you step by step through the creation of your budget. Also, there are various software programs to help you write a business plan, which include budget preparation. If you are knowledgeable about spreadsheet software (such as Quattro and Excel), they make budget number crunching easy work.

The process of putting the budget together, in my judgment, is more important than the budget itself. It is a process that is reflective of the values and philosophy of the entrepreneur who determines the content and the objectives of those creating it. The budget becomes a statement of goals and attitudes. Look at the individual line items and you will discover the priorities of the management or owner.

A well-crafted budget can be an important aid to you during your difficult first years. Think of a budget not as a list of expenses and income but as a positive thought process that forces you to make decisions and establish limits over your actions. It's a great strategy for success!

Budgets force you to think
Have you ever attempted to put a fantasy on paper? It's difficult. Wishful thinking and dreams can be illusive and as hard to define as some of our politicians are. A budget does not permit you to spend without regard to profits and losses. Every expenditure and every source of income is stipulated in the budget. If you give raises to your employees, it will change your budget. If you change your selling prices, your budget changes and so does your bottom line. A budget forces you to think through every action you take and how it affects your profits or losses.

Budgets force you to decide
If you have trouble making decisions, a budget will help you with the process. When you are creating a budget, you must make decisions—you must decide how much you are going to prioritize your money for which expenses and how important they are to you. A budget creates a perspective for you. A single expense may not seem like much but when viewed in relation to all the expenses, its importance to your business will be apparent.

Shades of gray disappear quickly in a business situation. You must make decisions—decisions about spending money, establishing prices, seeking certain profit margins and hiring and firing employees. Your budget is the financial plan of your business based on the results of your decisions.

A budget can also be a brake. Some entrepreneurs, once they have experienced a little success, become impatient for more. They succumb to the perils of overexpansion. A budget can quickly restore reality.

Break-Even analysis

Break-even analysis is an analytical tool used by economists and financial analysts to measure the profit potential of products and companies. It determines the minimum sales necessary to generate sufficient gross profit to cover your expenses. It's another way to see how much business you need to have to stay out of trouble and pay your bills.

The usual business expenses are of two types—fixed and variable. Fixed expenses (e.g., overhead) are costs the business will have to pay regardless of the amount of sales volume. These include most salaries, lease payments for the office or building, the insurance payment, the truck lease, installment debt, property and certain business taxes or any recurring expense that will continue at a "fixed" amount regardless of your level of sales or business activity.

In contrast, variable expenses are costs that change with changes in sales volume. Commissions are an example. If you are paying your sales staff five percent of sales, the percentage rate may remain constant but the dollars will change. The cost of goods is another item that varies. The more product you sell, the more product you will purchase.

An example of a simple computation of a break-even point is shown in Table 4. If your overhead or fixed expenses is $10,000 per month and your gross profit is 25 percent, to break even you must sell $40,000 per month to earn a gross profit of $10,000 to pay the expenses.

Any change in the gross profit will change your break-even point. If the gross profit changes to 50%, you will have to sell only $20,000 to cover your $10,000 of expenses. By contrast, if your gross profit decreases to 10%, your sales requirements jump to $100,000 to break even.

Table 4
Break-Even Analysis

Fixed Sales	Gross Profit (25%)	Expenses	Profit/Loss
$20,000	$ 5,000	$ 10,000	($5,000)
$30,000	$ 7,500	$ 10,000	($2,500)
$40,000	$10,000	$ 10,000	-0-
$50,000	$12,500	$ 10,000	$2,500

This is only the most rudimentary application of break-even analysis. You can find a great deal more about the subject in most business finance textbooks. It is a valuable management tool-check it out! Success in business is easy—just make a profit and avoid losses. If you use break-even analysis, you may prevent your business from losing your money due to excess overhead, too small a gross profit or insufficient sales volume.

Remember:
1. Staying in business is simple: just earn a profit! Because if you continually lose money, you will lose the business.
2. Assets that don't turnover can tie up your cash and reduce your business flexibility.
3. Pay attention to changes in your equity. Equity decreases with losses and a negative equity means insolvency.
4. Put together a budget and keep reviewing it.
5. Keep your overhead as low as possible.

Chapter 6
Unknown partners

It is tough enough to succeed in a new business, but with an employee dipping into your register it is even more difficult. Let us hope you never have an employee or an "unknown partner," who is stealing from you.

Your business can fail because of a dishonest employee. Any employee who steals from you, whatever the amount, is a hidden liability. I remember an audio equipment distributor that became bankrupt because the warehouse manager was stealing inventory and selling it to conspiring customers.

While we may wish to believe all employees are honest, it is naive to think so. Anyone in business should maintain a certain amount of distrust of others. There are many unscrupulous people in business, including vendors, customers and employees.

Reasons for "partnership"
Usually a dishonest employee will find some reason to justify the behavior. Valid or not, your employee may feel underpaid. As psychologists tell us, feelings of exploitation can lead to resentment and inappropriate behavior such as stealing.

Then there are amoral people, lacking ethics or a sense of morality who steal without guilt or concern. They need no justification. As talented as they may be, the risk of hiring and trusting such people is significant.

Drug and alcohol addiction may result in such a demand for money that any reasonable income or wage is not enough to sustain the addiction. If you suspect an employee with a drug or alcohol problem, see if your employee has a strong commitment to rehabilitation such as Alcoholics Anonymous or another form of treatment.

A troubled marriage with money problems can cause an employee to put aside his or her sense of honesty and give in to the temptation of a little extra cash. As an employer you cannot be involved in the marital problems of your employees, but you should be alert to changes in their behavior.

Your employees may become jealous of your success and lifestyle. They may feel they have contributed to the success of the firm and be tempted to steal their "share" of the profits. Since it is wise to be considerate of employees less fortunate than you, do not invite trouble by promoting a personal display of your new wealth.

If you pocket a little cash from the register or don't record a cash sale, your employees may feel free to do the same. Disregarding procedures and tax laws because you are the owner sends a powerful message to the employees. There are better ways and more honest ways of paying yourself.

How does it happen?

As you might expect, there are many ways employees can steal. For example, an employee may not record a cash sale and pocket the money. A sales clerk may sell merchandise to friends at "special" prices or even give away your inventory to friends. Some crooked employees make deals with customers while keeping the money.

If you have employees to whom you reimburse business expenses, be sure to check their reports for padded or phony expenses.

When I taught sales management I asked my students how many would cheat on their expense report. I am sorry to tell you that over half of each class said they would lie. When I asked why, I was told they assume everyone does, just as they assume everyone cheats on their tax returns.

If you deal with suppliers or vendors and have employees issuing purchase orders, be on the lookout for illegal payoffs of gifts or cash. Do not think for a moment this is harmless in any way. It is corruption, it is illegal and it is at your expense.

The practice is pervasive. It ranges from the shipping carton supplier who throws a few dollars to your shipping clerk to major suppliers who bribe your purchasing agents or buyers. Suppliers that resort to bribes as a sales strategy to get your business usually do so because the quality of their products is questionable or their prices are too high.

The former head of purchasing for three hospitals was convicted and sent to prison for taking over $160,000 in kickbacks from a supplier of X-ray film and supplies. In cahoots with the buyer, the vendor submitted bills to the buyer for nonexistent product. The conspiracy cost the hospitals millions of dollars.

Be certain you are not issuing checks to nonexistent suppliers. A common scam is a conspiracy to issue checks against phony bills submitted to your company. This is a favorite tactic of dishonest bookkeepers who may create fictitious companies to send you fraudulent bills. Besides vendor fraud, be alert for any unusual credits issued to customers. More than one bookkeeper has made deals with dishonest customers.

These examples are only a few of the many possibilities your employees, vendors and customers may do to rip off your business. And, just as I am not saying that everyone is dishonest, do not think every employee or everyone with whom you have business dealings is honest. Just be alert for errant or suspicious behavior that may cost you some of your money and even your business.

An ounce of prevention

Be honest in all your dealings. If you attempt to fudge your books, gouge a customer a little or cheat a vendor, you are sending a strong message to your employees or associates that you accept such behavior. It is an invitation to steal from you. If your employees know that you demand honesty, they will respect you for it. By doing so, you will find dishonest workers won't hang around. An honest environment will make them uncomfortable.

Learn enough about accounting procedures to put in a system

of checks and balances. Learn how to verify your paperwork. I am not suggesting you devote large amounts of time to doing so, but you can spot check invoices and bills which will alert everyone that you are on the lookout for theft. Employees are quick to sense an owner's ability to spot irregular activity; those individuals who are intent on lining their pockets will move on. I recall an employee who quit our business right after we installed a computer system to track inventory. He was not able to steal anymore.

Finally, remain alert to the possibility that you may have a dishonest employee on your staff. You may spare yourself the pain of employee theft if you keep accurate records, verify unusual transactions, avoid disorganization and a sloppy work environment and insist on hiring only "honest employees."

Remember:

1. Insist on honesty and check references on all employees you hire.
2. Keep accurate business records, especially inventory and cash.
3. Verify any "strange" transactions.
4. Set the right example—don't treat your business as your playground.
5. Watch for any change in the behavior of your employees.
6. Be alert to alcohol and drug problems.
7. Be alert to employee credit problems.
8. Watch out for cozy relationships between employees and suppliers.

PART THREE
Leadership

Leadership in a start-up business is unlike leadership in a mature organization. It demands a sense of urgency and an "action" style. As most start-ups lose money, definitive action is required to increase sales, acquire customers, develop products and collect money. Time is critical. The longer the losses continue, the closer to bankruptcy you are. Start-ups mandate action, not discussion.

I define "start-up leadership" as a style that creates an environment in which both the employees and owner realize a sense of urgency to establish the business on a sound footing as soon as possible. As the leader, the owner sets the philosophy of the business by example and attitude. The authority of the founder is upheld, but status or class distinction is not. Survival becomes a leader-directed team effort, with everyone realizing that if you don't make it, no one has a job or gets a paycheck.

Chapter 7
The people you hire, manage and lead

Since too much overhead can be dangerous to your business, begin by resisting the pressure and temptation of hiring too many employees. While the assistance of a staff is helpful, it is also costly and can drain your limited resources.

Any new entrepreneur who needs to surround himself or herself with unnecessary staff is headed for failure. As successful entrepreneurs will tell you, any fool can hire people and believe he or she is building a team for the future. Entrepreneurs need to surround themselves with action-oriented people and not contemplative consultants. Take the case of Al.

After many years as a business planner with a leading pump manufacturer, Al retired early to start a small distributorship of pumps and related parts. Experienced in management and finance, Al put together a business plan and arranged for office and warehouse space. To finance his business, Al borrowed against the equity in his home and pension. Because of his experience and contacts, he quickly found products to distribute. However, finding customers was not for Al as he had little sales background. He realized he needed help and hired Art, a former corporate colleague, as his vice president of marketing.

Art devoted nearly two months developing a complete market plan, leaving little time to accomplish anything else. Finally, after much frustration, Al told Art that planning was fine, but somebody better start selling something. Appearing surprised, Art did not understand the need to rush into the marketplace without a thorough analysis of customer needs. Up to this point, the company was selling to a handful of customers—not enough to stay in business. Al was running out of money and knew that if things did not quickly change, he must close the business.

Since Art was unable to make the transition from corporate planning to selling pumps, he quit. Al put everything aside and went out selling to save his company—and he succeeded. When the crisis passed, he hired a salesperson and tore up the market plan.

Many former corporate executives who have struck out on their own do not have a sense of urgency to get the new business on a solid foundation before the money runs out. Most are educated and trained in procedural-style management, which may be appropriate while running large corporations but is ill-suited to a start-up. Al was able to change. Not everyone is.

People management

Your first employees play a pivotal role in the survival of your business. They will be part of your company image. They will reflect your judgment. They will demonstrate your attitude. They will be your style of doing business.

As you start out, you can not afford to hire the wrong person. You must be careful. Don't encourage failure by sloppy or hasty hiring practices. The wrong employee can be costly. Remember Chapter 6 and the comments about dishonest help; they can put you out of business.

You are making an investment when you hire a new employee. He or she is a commitment of your time and money. Your decision must result in a productive employee who makes a contribution to your success. If you wind up with the wrong person, cut your losses as soon as possible. Don't be mislead by wishful thinking that the person will change. Most people don't.

Demonstrate your leadership skills by hiring the right people— recognizing that character, attitude and ambition are as important as education and experience.

Job descriptions
The purpose of a job description in a business is to clearly define the precise job an employee is to do. It should be as specific as possible. If you can tell a potential employee what you expect and require, it will also help avoid future misunderstandings.

Precise job descriptions force you to think. If you are going to take on the expense of an employee, you must know specifically what the person is going to do. For example, assume you recently started a small bookstore in an upscale Vermont college town. You are doing well and you find yourself falling behind with your paperwork. Bills are not getting paid on time, special orders for customers are being neglected and you are feeling that things are getting out of control. You need help. But what kind of help? Whom do you hire and what will the person do? These questions are the beginning of a job description.

A simple but effective method is to list the specific tasks the new employee will do. As you develop the list, attempt to estimate the time required each day to accomplish the routine or daily tasks. If you cannot fill up at least half the day, perhaps you really don't need anyone, but you are just feeling momentarily overwhelmed. Once you have completed the list and it seems practical, you have a job description and a defined understanding of the responsibilities of your new employee. Now look for someone with the talents and abilities to match your needs.

Avoid the type of job descriptions written for major corporations, as they usually are imprecise generalizations about the job. Ask your attorney about avoiding phrases such as "the ability to coordinate and deal with individuals on all levels of management" or "requires proficient communication skills with demonstrated leadership aptitude." Such phrases are not much help when you want to specify specific tasks and responsibilities.

As you build your business, you will begin to hire people to help you. Your choice will be a statement of your judgment and potential for success.

Delegate wisely

Delegation is an important part of management, but use common sense when deciding what to delegate. Attempt to find a balance. Too little delegation creates inefficiency and places impossible time demands on you, the owner. Too much delegation can result in a sloppy, poorly run company with excessive overhead; absentee management rarely works with start-ups.

Be careful about the overuse of accountants and consultants. If you are using your investment capital to support these professionals, you may be wasting your money. If you can't handle your finances and are uncertain about running your company, you won't last. Expensive professionals will not prevent you from failing, but they will present you with some hefty bills.

You need an accountant and a lawyer for certain tasks, but not to run your business. If you are having a tough time paying yourself, it does not make any sense to pay high hourly rates to someone take care of details you can do yourself. Why would you pay an accountant at least $100 an hour to balance your checkbook? If you don't know how to do basic financial tasks, educate yourself.

In a desperate act to survive, one owner I knew in a troubled business called in a consultant to save his firm from bankruptcy. After a series of meetings, the submission of a lengthy report of recommendations (which required money to implement) and a large consulting fee, the problem remained, but time and money were lost. Consultants are necessary in certain situations, but not as miracle workers or therapists.

Collective decision making
As the owner, you have the right to make all the decisions but should you? If you do, the mistakes will all be yours. Your emotions and personality quirks may too greatly influence your decisions.

Sharing the decision making responsibility with employees,

79

spouses or partners allows collective judgment that may result in better decisions—but may cause delay. How much you bring other people into the process depends on the quality of your human resources, but whatever approach you elect, the ultimate responsibility is still yours.

Individuals who have difficulty deciding things need to be careful about pushing that responsibility onto others as a way of avoiding decisions. Too much delegation of decision making can be foolhardy if you are the only one risking any money.

However, if you see yourself as a coach, with a team of employees that will make your success possible, then sharing opinions can be valuable to you. If you respect the opinion of your employees, you may respect their judgment as well. The autocratic military approach to management is passé. Usually, an intelligent, educated and well-informed employee will not work for a dictator. Although time consuming, collective judgment can reduce the risk of bad decisions and encourage employee loyalty and support.

How much should you delegate and involve your employees in deciding the issues of your company? It depends on you and your type of leadership style. Regardless of your style, there will always be some issues only you can decide. The larger the risk, the more the decision must be yours alone but the more you may need the views of others.

Impulse and intuition

You will occasionally see business books that promote intuition or listening to your inner vision for guidance.

To avoid bad decisions that can put you out of business, approach your problems with critical thinking and objectivity. Acting on impulse alone will stack the odds against you.

As I am not a psychologist or a spiritualist, I don't consider myself qualified to support or criticize the "intuitive approach to management." But, I do know from personal experience there have been times I have listened to "my gut" and things worked out. Decide for yourself!

Management or leadership?

Poor management and the lack of leadership are the leading causes of business failure. If you talk with those whose businesses have failed, you will discover how little they understood either.

Poor management has five main components: (1) not following through on activities started, (2) not caring to do your best, (3) not paying attention to details, (4) looking for shortcuts and (5) going through the motions without commitment.

If you cannot manage your personal affairs, managing your business will be even more difficult. If you lack managerial experience and you are uncomfortable with paperwork and financial details, it will be wise to recognize these shortcomings before risking your money in a business venture that requires such management skills.

Lack of leadership has six components: (1) a lack of vision, (2) a lack of dedication, (3) an inability to inspire others, (4) lacking trust in others, (5) failing to demonstrate honesty and a sense of ethics and (6) an inability to lead others to a common goal.

For some, leadership skills may be intuitive. For others, these skills may develop through training and experience. How you acquire these skills is not nearly as important as the fact that you must demonstrate enough leadership to succeed. To determine your leadership ability, look at how you approach your life and see how many "yes" responses you can provide to these five questions:

1. Do you take initiative?
2. Do you reach out to other people?
3. Are you an organizer?
4. Do others follow your suggestions?
5. Can you make things happen?

Starting a business from scratch requires leadership. It is creating something concrete from an idea. You motivate yourself. You convert a vision into a business. You convince others of your idea. You stubbornly commit to your goal. You ignore the nay sayers. You demonstrate your talents of leadership and persuasion.

To successfully launch a company, regardless of size, you need a lot of mental and physical energy, sustainable over long periods of time. As you may know, the start-up phase is very demanding. You will continually work, think, talk and plan your new venture. One moment will find you excited and happy over your plans and the next may haunt you with the terror of possible bankruptcy. These conflicting emotions can make your life difficult as you bounce between the optimistic vision of success and the nagging doubt of possible failure. Starting a business is a very new experience for most people. It is fraught with frustration and uncertainty. Even the newness of the situation can be overwhelming. One moment you are confident, the next fearful.

It's not an easy time. As you start your business, your leadership skills will set the foundation for the future. Your ability to stay focused, negotiate the best deals, hire the right people, make the correct decisions and instill confidence in others will be called upon daily. At this point and until things begin to sort out and settle down, you will find yourself doing more leading than managing.

"Micromanaging" and the need to control every little detail of the business is, in general, a poor management style and an obstacle to growth and success; however, when you have mortgaged your home or borrowed from friends and relatives, this is not the time to assume details are unimportant. Until you are on a solid footing, I advocate paying attention to detail and making sure things happen as planned. Without surplus cash reserves and a substantial customer base you have little margin of error. Put all the theories of management aside and rely on your common sense. A start-up is no place to experiment with various styles and techniques of management.

Remember:
1. You need a sense of urgency to make it in a small business today.
2. Action leadership is required.
3. Your best chance for survival is a leader-directed team effort.
4. Too much personnel too fast will put you out of business.
5. Be selective in hiring and don't hire anyone unless you know specifically what they are going to do.
6. Consider the needs of your business carefully when delegating.

7. If you don't like to make decisions, you shouldn't be in business.
8. Perhaps you should trust your gut.
9. Be careful about micromanaging, but don't neglect the details, especially in the beginning.

Chapter 8
Be a team leader,
not a soloist

A retired auto worker named Stuart leased a small gas station, becoming self-employed for the first time in his life. Unfortunately, he lasted in business just over eleven months before turning the station back to the oil company and moving to a mobile home park in Florida. He retired for the second time, only now as a bitter person with much less money.

Stuart failed because of his attitude. In his opinion, none of the people he hired wanted to work; all were lazy and shiftless. He told anyone who was willing to listen that there are few good auto mechanics today and he had to oversee or do all the repairs himself. Because of his constant criticism and distrust of his help, it became difficult for him keep employees. His views became a self-fulfilling prophecy as only his least skilled workers were willing to work for him.

His customers left him because of the many complaints of poor service and quality. The more his customers called his attention to poor workmanship and lack of courtesy by his employees, the more of a tyrant he became. Finally with most of his repair business gone and few repeat customers at the pumps, he gave up and cursed society for encouraging welfare and destroying the work ethic.

Stuart failed because of Stuart. Throughout his life, he never trusted anyone else's judgment. He elected himself monarch at home and exercised dictatorial powers over his family.

It was Stuart's opinion that no one was as smart as he, no one could do anything as well and most people were lazy. It was no surprise to his friends when he closed his station.

Total control

Unfortunately for Stuart, he did not understand that ego and leadership don't mix. He failed to realize that successful ventures are created through the coordinated efforts of an owner and employees. Even after his failure, Stuart denied any responsibility for what happened. He is still not convinced that unilateral decisions lead to a narrow and rigid management structure that fosters employee insecurity, high employee turnover, owner burnout, tension and failure.

"Total control" is a management style where the owner or manager keeps a tight reign over as many activities as possible. No decisions are permitted by anyone else, regardless of how minor the issue. Consequently, if all the decisions must wait for the boss, not much will get done in time. Such tight-fisted control is very inefficient.

Total control is symptomatic of insecurity. It is a lack of faith and trust in other people. It is repressive. As a management style, it leads to limited, if any growth. It discourages any human resource development and is devoid of teamwork. It focuses too much on small details rather than the big picture. It will eventually bring about total business failure.

If you don't trust your employees or their judgment and you are unwilling to allow them to assume some responsibility, you will be cheating yourself of the talent you are paying for. You can't build a one-person organization.

If you have the right people in your business, delegate the minor decisions to leave you time for the major ones. As the owner, you will always have the final say if you want it, but smart employees can give you some smart input. Take advantage of it.

Participatory management

During the early 1900s Frederick Taylor developed the concept of "scientific management" as a means of increasing productivity. He became well known as the "father of scientific management," famous for his time and motion studies. He advocated a management philosophy where the employee as a person did not matter, only their productivity.

Taylor did not encourage management to seek or accept input from the work force. His views erected a barrier between management and labor that still exists in some companies. Today, however, more enlightened and informed business leaders view their labor force as an asset, not an extension of equipment. They also use a more participatory style of management.

If you take the time to hire the right people and invest in their training, by all means, listen to them and encourage their ideas and participation. To be an effective leader you must become proficient at team building. Sole control and authority over all matters, without input or feedback, can easily lead to errors of judgment. Taylor's approach, while effective nearly 100 years ago, does not work well today with literate and educated employees.

Motivation: Without fear

In the past, to prod employees to greater productivity fear was used as a tool of discipline and motivation. Repressive management in some firms still use the fear of termination to keep workers in line. In fact, some sales managers frequently threaten to fire poor performers unless they improve immediately.

Fear works as a method of control and will force people to comply with orders, but it is weak management. Any fool can yell and threaten to fire, but what appears as compliance is really a begrudged minimal effort—effort performed with suppressed hostility.

If you believe as a small business owner that fear demonstrates power and authority, you are right. But it does not develop any form of team spirit or collective purpose. If you feel you must resort to loudly spoken commands, rigid rules and no tolerance for disagreement, either you are not managing well or you have hired the wrong employees.

But there is a better way: motivation can be accomplished by an appeal to self-interest. It may be with money, with privileges or with recognition. The employee must believe that if he or she follows your directions and works for your self-interest, you will reward their self-interest.

The paycheck alone is not motivation. It is a retainer. But additional money can be a motivator. Do not make the mistake, however, of thinking that money motivates everyone. With his concepts of scientific management, Taylor relied on increased earnings through the piece-rate system as a way of boosting production. Industrial psychologists have found that not all workers respond to such stimulation.

Recognition motivates many people more often than money. In fact, awards and motivational products are big business today. Acknowledgment and peer awareness of accomplishments are powerful motivators. Plaques, titles, size of office and special parking spots are just some of the offerings of management to motivate performance and loyalty.

Fear has shown itself to be a short-term motivator at best. It is a technique of desperate and incompetent management. Successful owners know you cannot build an efficient organization with continual threats of firing. Employees who tolerate such treatment are usually insecure, unimaginative, docile people who follow enough orders to get by.

As an entrepreneur, if you have hired honest and industrious employees, appeal to their self-interest and get them excited about "their" company and their future.

Remember:

1. Autocracy or one-person rule does not work well in business.
2. Recognize your employees as team members.
3. Fear does not work.
4. To motivate, appeal to each employee's self-interest.

Chapter 9
Stay focused

Are you organized? You will not stay in business long if you manage with chaos and confusion. You will find it costly, wasteful and demoralizing; in short, it begs failure. Your success is going to hinge upon your ability to remain organized, regardless of the financial and emotional pressures your business places on you.

Unfortunately, there are people who become frantic and rush about in a frenzy whenever they must complete some project or major task. These people are like the center of a hurricane; surrounded by turbulent forces, they create confusion and clutter and in time, disaster. Any semblance of order and efficiency disappears in such an environment. Mistakes are common, customers are frustrated, employees are confused and direction is nonexistent.

Lack of direction
Don't waste your time on nonessential tasks or you will have difficulty in accomplishing the activities vital to your survival, such as making collection calls or paying bills. If you do squander your time, you may feel sorry for yourself—complaining about too much to do and too little time to do it.

As an employee, you may be able to survive with such poor

work habits, but as the owner of a business, you won't. You are responsible to chart the direction of your company, establish schedules, determine priorities and strive to meet your goals.

With your life savings at risk, your sense of focus will be critical to your survival and success. You cannot waste your time on tasks and nonsense that take you away from your goals.

Whenever you are feeling the pressure to be sidetracked with such activities, reflect and ask yourself just what will this activity do to help you accomplish your goals and major objectives. Ask yourself, "What is my most important task at the moment?" During the critical start-up phase as you are struggling to stop the cash drain and to become profitable, remember your time is limited—and every action you take must be to grow your business.

As a suggestion, when you feel the pressure of too much to do, back away, take a few deep breaths and prepare a priority list. It helps to slow down and approach your problems one at a time. Do you recall the material on procrastination? Watch out for too many incomplete projects.

With a lack of direction you accomplish little. Spend some of your time planning the direction and objectives of your company. Establish what is important for survival and which of your pressing needs demands your immediate attention. Then pace yourself. A successful business leader is skillful at establishing priorities and deadlines and allocating time.

Working hard and working smart are not the same
There are people who work hard, but accomplish little. They are

always pressed for time, busy, frustrated and ineffective. Somehow, they confuse hard work with productive work. You have probably heard that breaking rocks with a sledge hammer in a prison yard is hard work but not productive. Aim to work smart as well as hard. Don't waste your time polishing your desk when you should be making sales calls.

Working too hard is ineffective
Don't exhaust yourself with work. If you get too tired you will not be alert and your decisions may not be the best. If you run yourself down as a result of continual, stressful overwork, your drive and enthusiasm will wane and you may even become ill. Furthermore, your emotions may begin to take charge and you will lose your objectivity.

As you move your new company through its critical first years, you must be at your best to deal with what will seem to be an unending list of problems. Fatigue can place you in a precarious position. It can lead to poor thinking, irrationality, impatience and problem paranoia. The effects of fatigue can lead to failure and even self-destructive behavior. It is an insidious enemy— one you can ill afford as an entrepreneur. Pace yourself and know when to stop working.

Alcoholic's Anonymous uses the acronym "HALT" to warn against becoming "hungry, angry, lonely and tired," as any one condition will affect your emotional stability, the lack of which can put you out of business.

How to work smart
Working smart is the ability to size up work activities in terms of their importance and then to do them most efficiently in the

least amount of time. As an entrepreneur, you are an economic resource with absolute limitations on your time. In fact, time is the only resource in your venture you can't change. Because of the limits on your time and the unlimited demand for it, you need to make many choices each day. For every task you do, there is at least one you cannot choose to do because there isn't enough time. As you can imagine, frustration and anxiety may easily develop from such a situation.

When we feel overworked and under pressure, we may blame these feelings on the lack of time, but very often it is not time; it is our use of it.

How do you get more time? You apply the principle of multiplication—that is, you extend your talents and your judgment through others. To do so, you train your employees. You sharpen your delegation skills. You remain aware of the dangers of attempting to dominate every situation. You sit on your ego. You ask for and accept help from others. You work to develop a team approach in your business with shared obligations and responsibilities. Part of working smart is accomplishing tasks through others.

Technology also permits us to work more efficiently. Consider the amount of computer software that is available today to help the small business owner operate effectively. For example, there are programs that help you write an entire business plan. There are a multitude of other programs ranging from form letters to accounting. Why reinvent the wheel? Don't waste your time with chores best left to technology.

If you find it difficult to allocate your time during the day or if you are easily distracted, consider the following approach. For one week, start each day with a list of your most pressing tasks. List them in order of importance with an estimate of the amount of time needed for each. If you're attempting to squeeze two days of work into one, you have a problem. Study the list each day and then decide what you can postpone, eliminate or ask someone else to do. As you go through each day, write down your activities. At the end of the day compare the lists. You may be surprised at how much time you waste on minor issues.

There is a management principle called Parkinson's Law that says, "Work expands to fill the time available," which means if you (or your employees) have spare time or act as if you do, the following time wasters could result: (1) questionable make-work activities will fill up the time or (2) work that could have been done in a shorter amount of time will end up taking maybe twice as long to do. You can not afford to waste your time, nor can your employees. Remember, you pay for it. To have an efficient organization, the efficiency must begin with you.

Are you running the business or is it running you?

If the everyday running of your business is crisis management, something is wrong, because crisis management as a daily diet is a crisis within itself. When such conditions exist, the business has taken charge and is managing the owner. Although, crisis management is correct for the occasional crisis that will occur, as a daily management style, it is not. If everything is a crisis, how do you plan? How do you establish goals and set priorities? You don't. It is a counterproductive way to manage any type of organization. Failure is only a matter of time.

Ask yourself these questions. Do you spend most of each day

95

solving problems? Are you constantly responding to a complaint, a last-minute deadline or the latest urgent problem? Do you have the feeling you are being pulled in many directions all at once? Yes responses indicate a crisis management style.

If you seem to suffer from too much to do, not enough time to do it and whatever you do is always late, it is time to question who is in charge. With such conditions, it would be wise to look at your management style. If your days are filled with one crisis or problem after another, it will be difficult for you to maintain a positive attitude about your business.

Do you remember the story of Helen in Chapter 4? If you recall, she was the problem, not her employees, not her customers and not the bank. As Helen worked in a constant state of confusion, bouncing from task to task in a state of frenzy, her personal management style created the majority of her problems. She would forget to deposit her payroll taxes and wind up with a fine and penalty. She continually made errors with her paperwork, even to the extent of not billing customers for certain jobs. Consequently, most of her daily routine was spent putting out fires or crisis management. No one was happy. Employees never stayed on the job very long. Creditors became impatient with false promises and customers grew tired of questionable quality.

How do you know if your business is running you? If the majority of your time is spent reacting to someone else's actions, you are not the boss. The business is. If you have lost the latitude of planning your schedule and determining your priorities, you are not in charge. Every business has problems that must be promptly attended to, but if the problems are created by your management style, it is time to seek help before you lose the business. There are many small business development centers at local universities and colleges that can be of help. There is also a volunteer group of seasoned business leaders called "SCORE" (Service Corps of Retired Executives) with local chapters in every state.

How to stay on course

A well-thought-out business plan is invaluable for staying on track with your goals. When you have invested your savings or borrowed heavily, it may be difficult to remain calm and objective during those times when you feel your world is falling apart. Under such pressure, it is easy to lose sight of your goals and allow the latest problem to mushroom in your mind. To survive the tough times of getting established, you need to develop realistic business plans and expectations. Apply these suggestions:

1. Don't rely on some miracle to solve your problems. They do happen but not under your control or schedule.
2. Plan for the downside. If your project does fail, do you have any kind of backup position? How much of a loss can you weather and stay in business? If your plans don't work out and you know you can survive, the knowledge will do wonders for your sense of security.
3. Don't fall for pie in the sky planning based on wishful thinking. Your business plans must be real! If you are projecting a million dollars in sales, can you identify where it is coming from? Your plans will be more realistic if you can be specific as to how are you going to get to your goal. Fuzzy thinking can be costly.
4. Follow the suggestions outlined in the chapters on money

and in the Appendix. Forecast your cash needs. Plan for a surplus or shortage. Don't leave your cash situation to chance. Once you begin chasing dollars to cover overdrafts it's tough to feel confident.

5. Establish target dates to complete projects or tasks. Firm dates help to build discipline.

6. Put your plans in writing. Granted, it takes time; however, a new business has little margin of error and your plans must make sense. They must be real not fantasy.

7. Use to-do lists—lots of to-do lists. When you are keeping many balls in the air, it is easy to forget one.

8. Take some quiet time at least once a week to reflect on your progress. As any therapist will tell you, our creative juices flow best when we are quiet. It is during such times that answers to some of our problems emerge. Work at reducing your anxieties—tension can be counter-productive.

9. Reflect and review your progress (or lack of it) versus your plans. Circumstances surrounding your business may have changed. Your business plan may need modification. An effective plan is flexible.

10. Are you still enthused? Are you doing what you want to? Are you still optimistic about the future? Do you still believe in your goals? If you wonder, have doubts or have lost your zest for your business, stop to look carefully at how you are managing your business and yourself.

Take stock of yourself. Check your motives, Be careful about becoming overtired and overly stressed. Fatigue, physical and emotional, can raise havoc with your efficiency and judgment.

A personal note
During a difficult period, approximately two years after starting one of my companies, Adams Magnetic Products, I learned the value of just stopping and putting my emotions on hold. Due to a series of blunders and poor judgment, my company was headed for extinction. I had overestimated the market for my product and seriously underestimated my cash requirements. I was being sued by so many creditors I lived in fear of the phone and certified mail. In addition, I was losing customers because of late deliveries and quality problems. I was at the point of throwing in the towel, but I did not have enough money to file for bankruptcy.

At the time of my business problems, I was also experiencing personal problems. As an escape from my emotional nightmare, I began reading Emerson and other transcendentalists as well as some works on Eastern mysticism and spiritualism. I learned that you cannot be effective and solve problems if you are stressed out and emotionally distraught. I believe a turning point in my fortunes occurred when out of desperation for some emotional peace, I informed my partner I was taking a week off and going away and shutting out the world.

For one week I did not make a phone call or speak to anyone about my business problems. I thought, I read, I slept and I "let go." By the end of the second day I felt less nervous. At the end of the week I felt some internal peace for the first time in two years.

I returned to my company refreshed and more insightful about my problems. I took each day as it came and trained myself to shut off my problems each Friday and force myself to be "quiet" during the weekend. It worked. I slowly solved the problems one at a time and over the next three years my company gradually paid its creditors, gained new customers and became profitable. I learned many lessons from that experience. Last year, Adams Magnetic Products celebrated its eighteenth year in business, as a successful business.

If you are experiencing a similar situation, try my approach. You can't deal with your pressures and problems if you are in a frantic state of mind. Step back and cut up your problems into little bites. It works!

Remember:
1. Leadership mandates organization. You cannot stay in business with chaos and confusion.
2. Being in business is being in the driver's seat. You can't be a vessel without a rudder.
3. Ask yourself, "What is my most important task at the moment?" Don't waste your time polishing your desk when you have sales calls to make to your customers.
4. Remember HALT. Don't get hungry, angry, lonely or tired.
5. Work hard and smart.
6. Learn to use the power of multiplication with your time. Use other people and technology.
7. To have an efficient organization, the efficiency must begin with you.
8. Crisis management as a daily diet is a crisis in itself.
9. Keep your business plan flexible.

Chapter 10
Good housekeeping leads
to quality and success

At one time I worked with the president of a medium-sized
company who claimed that he could sense if a business was
headed for trouble by its housekeeping.

In his opinion, if a company's offices, warehouse or plant were
dirty, sloppy and disorganized, the business was probably in
trouble. I agree with him. If a business is a mess on the outside,
it will be on the inside—that is, its financial records and quality
control procedures, if any, will probably be sloppy and inaccurate and its management will lack pride. But whatever the
problems, the housekeeping of a business lies within management's control.

Appearance is everything
We form conclusions about others by the way they look. To
prove it, a New York market research firm conducted a study on
the importance of appearance in obtaining an appointment or
interview. Ten males in their twenties, dressed in jeans and
sweatshirts, fanned out to ten preselected corporate offices, each
attempting to get an appointment with the president of the
company. In every instance, the receptionists curtly rebuffed the

young men, indicating the executives were busy people and offered no possibility of a future appointment.

Dressed from Brooks Brothers the following week, the same individuals were sent to the same offices. The responses varied from an offer of help to an immediate interview. Each young man was treated with respect and courteousness. This interesting, although not scientific study, presents a convincing argument that our physical appearance greatly influences how we are judged and treated by others.

And as we judge people, we also judge businesses by the way they appear to us. If you manage an unkempt business or institution, you are making a personal statement about your leadership style. If your company is dirty, cluttered and generally disorganized, your employees, customers and vendors may quickly come to the opinion you lack pride.

If you do not care about the physical appearance and efficiency of your company, who will? Just because you pay your employees well does not mean they will devote their energies to making the place shine. If you don't care, why should they? Pride in a business must start with the owner. You can trace the lack of pride right to the top. Even new employees who arrive on the job beaming with enthusiasm will soon lose it under such conditions. Pride is profitable and contagious—practice it!

Lack of pride is contagious, too. If your employees have a bad impression of your company, so will your customers. Physical shabbiness and a disorganized appearance are not good customer relations. Image has a very loud voice and unless you have a monopoly, you will be wise to try to protect yourself from failure by working to create an efficient and professional appearing company.

To do so, does not require that you spend a fortune on decor. It requires that you create a neat, clean and organized environment with offices and other facilities cleaned daily, windows washed, lights working and fresh paint. These simple basics say you care about your company and you care about your employees' surroundings.

Your suppliers will judge you on your housekeeping. When they extend credit they are making an investment in your company. If you look as if you are about to close your doors, they may get a little nervous. If you are to survive, you need their support and the best possible credit terms. A successful business friend once told me that his suppliers are more important to his firm than his customers. It was his opinion that it is easier to replace a customer than a vendor. I think he is right.

The importance of accurate records

If your paperwork is inaccurate, sloppy and disorganized, you are creating an ideal situation for mistakes. Do you have any idea just how easy it is to pay a bill twice if the paperwork is not correct? Or how easy it can be to forget to invoice a customer? When it comes to customer or vendor bills, paperwork control equates to cash management. Paperwork must be treated with respect and not as a bothersome detail.

Poor and sloppy recordkeeping can be a cause of business failure. If you are not up to date on the costs of your operation, your sales figures or your cash flow, you are placing your company at an unnecessary risk. If you need help in keeping your paperwork straight, get help. Don't gamble in order to achieve some false economy. Don't overlook technology. The right software programs can do wonders in keeping your records under control. Sound financial management and sloppy or careless administration rarely coexist.

A $20-million blunder

Years ago, I watched a 10-year-old, $20-million company gradually slide into bankruptcy and on the auction block in less than three years. At its prime, the company employed over 250 and operated two manufacturing plants. It had developed a substantial customer list and a reputation for having low prices, too low to make a profit.

Throughout its troubled history, there were constant rumors of cash problems. But, regardless of the latest story, the company somehow managed, although always late, to pay its bills and keep its doors open. When the filing for bankruptcy occurred, no one was surprised.

I believe the path to bankruptcy started the day the company opened. The management always sought shortcuts and band-aid approaches to problems—so much so that the accounting records were a mess, mistakes were common with customer orders and products were routinely returned because of poor quality. Who was to blame? According to management, it was the employees.

The company was a mess, in more ways than one. Throughout the plant, the warehouse and the offices there was dirt and debris. The computer center looked more like a storage center for refuse than the nerve center of the company. In every office,

the filing cabinets and desks were covered with loose documents. Even the employee lunch room was unappetizing with
the odor of stale and discarded food. The factory floor was
usually littered with semifinished product and raw materials.
Mistakes were common. Quality control was talked about, but
never implemented. As the company faltered, more and more
shortcuts were taken with cheaper manufacturing materials.
Questionable invoicing mistakes appeared routinely and quality
assurance disappeared altogether. Attempts by employees to
notify the owners of problems were ignored. Any suggestions by
employees were pushed aside as if it were none of their business.

Downsizing was forced upon the company. A year before the
final collapse, management became desperate for cash.

Finally one morning, when the employees arrived for work, they
were told by security personnel that the company had closed
and they should remove any personal items and leave the pre-
mises. They were told their paychecks would be mailed. As you
might expect, there were a lot of angry people.

Two months later competitors and bargain hunters walked
throughout the plant waiting for the auctioneer to start the
bidding. By noon of that day, it was all over.

This business tragedy did not need to happen. The company's
outward appearance accurately reflected that the company was
sick. With care and professionalism, errors could have been
prevented. For example, a production run of 75,000 units at a
cost of $60,000 was returned by a customer because the wrong
product labels had been glued to each unit. To solve the problem, three hourly employees spent a full week hand scrapping

the wrong labels from all 75,000 pieces. This was a costly error that could have been avoided with a simple inspection procedure during production.

This was a business disaster that cost employees their jobs, suppliers millions of dollars and the founders their company. As the company slid into ruin, management missed many opportunities to change things. They could have corrected enough mistakes to halt the decline. Yet, they didn't.

If management had cared enough about quality to take steps to clean up and prevent messes, they could have avoided most of the problems and probably the bankruptcy.

If you care enough about your products, service and business, your employees will share your pride, too. If you don't care, don't expect your employees to either.

Remember:
1. We are judged by our appearance and so are our businesses.
2. If you don't care about the physical appearance and efficiency of your business, who will?
3. If your employees get a bad impression of your business, what will your customers think?
4. Caring about quality is the foundation of success.
5. Work to instill pride throughout your business.
6. Quality management starts with good housekeeping.

Chapter 11
Be assertive:
Ask, say no and follow up

I think saying no to people must be equal to the distasteful task of asking for something. Most of us do not like being placed in a situation where we must say no to a request or ask something of someone. Either can make us feel uncomfortable. Yet, the ability to say no without alienation and the skill to persuade others to accommodate us are talents we must have for the success of our business.

Being assertive—what it means

Assertive people do not have a problem saying no. They feel secure in doing so and are willing to accept the risk of confrontation. They have the courage of their convictions. They know the price of leadership is sometimes standing alone.

To be assertive is to assert your rights, to express yourself, to stand up for yourself and what you believe in. It is being able to declare who you are, what you feel and what you think. It involves openness, honesty and firmness. It is an active approach to the problems of life as compared to a passive approach. People who are not assertive, tend to be passive, inhibited and submissive—not admirable qualities for an entrepreneur.

In contrast, being too assertive borders on aggression. Aggressive behavior infringes on the rights of others, attacks them and puts them down. It is destructive, hurts people and causes them to feel badly. Aggressive people are often defensive and seldom have many friends.

Assertiveness is acting in your own best interest. It is the ability to function at ease in a variety of personal relationships. It is the ability to function as a leader and manager.

Assertiveness is setting limits on time and energy. It is having the inner strength to withstand criticism, put-downs or anger. It is expressing honest feelings in a comfortable manner. It means having the ability to disagree, to show anger, to show affection, to admit fears and to be spontaneous, all with self-confidence.

Assertiveness is the ability to express your opinions and to have the courage to cause change. Assertive people rarely play the role of victim. Assertive behavior is a positive attitude and a self-affirmation that places value on the other people in your life. It can lead to a happier and more fulfilling life.

Benefits of learning to be assertive
The most important benefit of assertiveness is freedom from anxiety. With the amount of stress you will have from your business, anything that lessens tension and anxious feelings will be beneficial. Developing assertiveness tends to reduce the anxieties you may feel in relationships with others. Worrying too much about what you are going to say and do in handling any particular situation will make you anxious. Learning appropriate assertive responses can reduce those anxious feelings.

Another important benefit is greater emotional freedom. When we feel restricted and limited in our freedom to respond to others, we are limiting our personal freedom. People who "walk on eggs" with others are not spontaneous. No one should be subject to the domination, whim and aggression of others. When you are able to be assertive, you are free from these aggressive or emotional traps.

Becoming assertive is not easy. If you have a passive personality and wish to be more assertive, you can learn to do so. Many have. But it will take effort and a sustained desire to do so. If you feel you have problems in communicating or feeling confident enough to be open and honest with others, you may need some training. If you have the time and money, the easiest way is to see a psychologist specializing in such behavior therapy. However, as you probably need every dollar for your business, you may have to rely on other ways to learn how to become more assertive.

You may wish to check with your local community college. If you cannot locate or attend a course, visit your library or local bookstore. You will find a variety of titles on the subject. Reading a few books on the subject could be a cost-effective way to build assertiveness into your life.

Here a few suggestions that may help you learn how to be more assertive:
1. You must have a sincere desire to change your behavior.
2. To change, you must be willing to assume emotional risk such as rejection or anger by others.
3. Be prepared to surprise those who know you as they will not be expecting your new responses.

4. Start gradually, take small risks at first and develop confidence in your ability to handle the challenge.
5. Be easy on yourself and accept the fact that there is no perfect response to every situation.
6. Practice being fair and honest in your dealings with others.
7. Don't use gimmicks or pat answers to solve problems.
8. Value yourself.
9. Don't be upset if everyone does not like you. Do you like everyone?

If you do try to change, learning new behavior skills will require effort and practice. It will not be easy; I know from experience. Even today, after consciously applying the suggestions I offer you, I must remind myself to be assertive when confronted with uncomfortable situations. It took me months of practice to "step up to the plate" and be forthright and completely honest in expressing my views and thoughts to friends, customers and suppliers.

I learned that "yes-ing" only postpones problems as no one respects false promises. My best relationships are those that have been built on truth and mutual respect. How do you feel when someone has promised you something and fails to fulfill that promise? I remember a fellow professor, who whenever students complained about a grade, would say that he would look into it, implying that perhaps the grade might be changed. When it was not, the disappointed students became angry. He was denied tenure because too many students filed complaints. His lack of candor and firmness hurt his career.

The major benefit, however, will be more direct and open communication with whomever you deal.

Aggression

There is a fine line between being assertive and aggressive. In certain situations it is easy to mistake aggression for assertion; both protect your own rights but aggression tramples others' rights, too. If you react out of anger, it is probably aggression. The trite phrase you can win the battle but lose the war is true when we act aggressively toward one another. If we do so to our employees, they may have no choice but to tolerate it, but we will neither inspire them nor obtain their loyalty with such behavior. In fact, aggressive acts toward employees, customers, suppliers or our friends will be costly to us in the long run.

Anybody who has been berated or been subjected to some form of public humiliation is not apt to forget it. We must be careful about crossing the line from assertiveness to aggressiveness. Passive people who are attempting to become assertive may overreact and become aggressive. Be careful, it is not all right to vent your anger to your employees or anyone else. There are people who delight in "telling others off," but do not be one of them. You will need the help of many to make your business a success.

I know of a modestly successful company operated by two brothers who are so aggressive toward each other they cannot maintain offices in the same building. They conduct their business relationship over the telephone and fax. They fought as children and have never stopped. It is a case of sibling rivalry that did not disappear with puberty or adulthood. It is amazing their business has survived. They are both talented and bright, but they do not share the same values and rarely agree on a common set of objectives. They function as partners only when necessary. Both contribute to the business, but only enough to assure that it continues.

One of the brothers confuses assertiveness with aggression and delights in "fighting" with suppliers who tolerate it as they need the business. In his attempts to be assertive, he allows his emotions to dominate. His aggressive and ego-driven attitude does not permit a cordial partnership between the brothers. The other brother reacts emotionally to the disagreements, which does not help the situation.

They have paid a price as the business is stagnate and has never reached its potential. If they had tried to foster a relationship of sharing and mutual trust without concern for bruised egos, they might have developed a business ten times its present size. A sense of leadership and purpose is missing in this firm because of the partners' anger, insecurities, inflated egos and emotional dishonesty. Dysfunctional relationships do not belong in any business partnerships.

The ability to ask

Starting a business is an innovative and enterprising act. It requires courage, faith in the future and assertive behavior to make it happen. The very act of launching the business requires the ability to ask things of others. Asking means taking the initiative. It is not a passive activity. It is putting forth an effort to make something happen. It also means accepting rejection, which will occur from time to time.

As an entrepreneur you must ask much of others and you cannot be hesitant to do so. If your business is to be a reality, you must ask others to have faith in you. You must ask others to trust you. You must ask others to lend you money. You must ask people to invest with you. You must ask potential customers to buy from you. You must ask your customers to pay you. As a business owner, you will spend much of your time asking others to do things for you.

As I wrote in the chapters on money, asking to be paid by your customers should be pretty routine. If you dislike asking for your money, don't extend credit. Remember, however, asking for money becomes easier after asking a few customers a few times and getting checks in the mail. You may even come to enjoy the task. Customers who are slow in paying their bills expect to be asked. And it is those who ask who are paid. Do not assume customers will automatically send you what they owe you; they too, may have cash flow problems. Asking for what is owed to you is not begging.

Asking customers to buy is also difficult for some business people. A customer may have an obligation to pay you, but they do not have an obligation to buy from you. Expect to hear no frequently. In the following chapters on promotion and sales, you will read about the many ways of asking customers to buy from you. Selling is challenging and necessary if you are to stay in business. With a little training, most anyone can master the basics.

Here are a few tips. First of all, any no you get is not about you as a person; it is about the product or service you are offering. Furthermore, you must ask and ask and ask. If you are building your business by selling to other businesses, remember this expression: People want to do business with people who want to do business. If you have trouble asking for the order, how serious are you about it? If you cannot bring yourself to do so, then go into the mail order business or open a parking lot.

But you can learn to ask. Anyone can. Put aside those childhood instructions of being told it is not polite to ask. Forget about feeling hurt or rejected if you are told no. Focus on the positive image of your successful business. Hold that image as a goal above any obstacle or resistance and believe that your determination will succeed. If you do not ask, you will never know.

Saying no

I have discussed this subject with other business owners and most share the view that learning to say no is one of the most difficult things to learn in business. Yet, you must, because if you agree to every demand made of you, your business will soon become unmanageable. We must learn to say no to our employees, our customers and our suppliers.

Why do we hate to say no? We dislike confrontation. When we reject a request we are never quite sure of the response we may get. It may range from understanding to outright hostility. We never know. Employees can become bitter and quit, customers can stop buying from us and suppliers can stop selling to us. Yet, we know we need to say no. If we have children, we are familiar with the need to say no. We say it out of love and necessity. We must do the same with our business.

Employees

If you have employees, they will make demands on you. When you start out, your initial employees may be understanding about your need to watch every dollar. But, as your business expands and money becomes more plentiful, you may expect the requests for raises and benefits to start. How much of your resources you wish to give to your employees is your decision, but it is impossible to grant every employee demand, from a pay increase to time off, and stay in business.

As much as you may try, there are few secrets in a small business. If you are generous to a particular worker, others will expect similar treatment. If employees think you are making money, expect them to knock on your door. As an employer, you will quickly come to the conclusion of the need to say no. Saying no to a valuable worker is difficult, but there are times you must, even when the person threatens to quit. You must never allow yourself to be held hostage to threats of quitting. If you establish a pattern of acquiescence, it is going to be difficult to reverse it.

Most major corporations have established employee policies and procedures to discourage arbitrary demands and to serve as a basis for saying no. Such procedures outline the basis for pay increases, vacations and fringe benefits. Each type of job has a description and an established pay range. Such written procedures avoid conflict and define the rules for all to see. Small businesses should also have such job descriptions and pay ranges.

Most employees expect reasonable and just treatment. Employee loyalty develops from consistent and fair employee policies. Discrimination of any type will lead to hostility and problems. Be fair and honest with your employees and you will find it easy to say no to any unreasonable demand.

Customers
Customers will ask you for lower prices and better terms. Your

customers want you to stay in business, but they want you to sell to them at the lowest price possible. And they will be quick to tell you if your competitor offers a better deal. If you meet every competitive price challenge, bankruptcy is inevitable.

Saying no to an unprofitable sale is basic good business. Overly aggressive salespersons do not always understand the need for profit to remain in business—for them a sale is sacred. Volume is king. Once you have established your minimum price margins, hold fast. Price cutting to make a sale or to hold on to a customer may be necessary on occasion, but as a routine it will lead to losses. Once you start to respond to price demands, it will be difficult to stop. You will need a stable price policy to maintain your profit margins.

Customers do not stop at demanding price concessions; they want all types of special treatment. They want free sample merchandise, free installation, free delivery, free replacements and free credit. There is no end to the number and type of requests they can think of to ask.

And, if you are dependent on one or two customers for the bulk of your business, it can be a dangerous situation if they make unreasonable demands because the loss of such customers can jeopardize your business.

In Chicago, a small wire rack manufacturing company, was approached by a major retail chain and asked to make a variety of racks for them to sell in their stores. The owner was delighted as his customers were, for the most part, slow-paying smaller stores.

His business boomed. The large chain, within a few months, absorbed most of the output and dominated the company. The existing small customers were purposely neglected, with a who-needs-them attitude.

As the owner entered his second year of selling to the chain, however, he found them increasingly difficult to deal with as they began to demand unreasonable price concessions. He knew that without their business, he would have to close. His company had become captive to its biggest customer.

At the time of the next contract negotiation, he was firmly told that without further price reductions, they would look for another supplier. He said no as further concessions were impossible. But it was too late—he lost the customer and his business.

Suppliers
Don't say yes to a supplier to be accommodating or to impress them with your purchasing power. With limited resources, you should buy only what you need. Business purchasing should be based on objectivity not emotion. If you cannot make money selling it or use it to make money, you do not need it. Even if your most important supplier pressures you to buy beyond your needs, don't! A no will always be respected when you pay the bill on time. It makes no sense for any reputable supplier to push you out of business by forcing too much inventory on you.

Follow-up
The bane of the majority of salespersons and job applicants, is the reluctance to follow up. Do you dislike to press for an answer or decision for fear you may be intruding or perceived as "pushy"? If you do, change immediately. Remember the familiar

sayings "out of sight out of mind" or "the squeaky wheel gets the grease"? Well, they are true. Do you always do everything the first time you are asked? I know I do not, much to the displeasure of my wife.

When you follow up you are demonstrating a seriousness of purpose. Our request, whatever it may be, is not a whim. Following up makes a statement about you; it says you are persistent, it says you are goal oriented and it says you are willing to make the effort to get what you want.

When I was vice president of marketing for International Tape Cartridge Corporation, one of my responsibilities was to organize and develop a national sales force. In doing so, I followed my personal rule that if anyone I interviewed did not follow up with me at least one time, I would not hire them. Why? It showed no initiative on their part. If a salesperson cannot follow up to see if they are a candidate for a job, will he or she follow up to make a sale or get a new customer? My system worked for me since few of those I hired failed.

In selling, as you will read later on, follow-up is critical to success. A major complaint about salespeople from purchasing agents is the lack of follow-up—a failure to follow through on requests made of them, a failure to keep the customer informed on order status and even a failure to make a sales call.

Collection activity is also follow-up. If you want your credit customers to pay you on time, they must know you will follow up. In a sense you are training them. If they know that whenever their account is past due you will be calling, faxing or sending a note, you will be paid sooner than a creditor who does not follow up. As you read earlier, if you want your money, ask for it—that is following up.

As you build your business, use follow-up to your advantage. You may realize that following up is a problem for many people. If there is someone or something you want, follow up; your competitor may not. Use your initiative to gain the advantage.

When I entered the academic world, I was hired to develop the business school at Ramapo College. One of my responsibilities was to recruit and hire faculty. In doing so, I was motivated to hire one particular professor, whose qualifications were equal to those of other applicants. Why? Because he contacted me every week for almost two months checking on the status of his application. I viewed his persistence as an indication of his motivation to teach at our college. I was right. Twenty years later, he is a highly respected full professor. He never lost his motivation and dedication to teaching. He followed up!

Remember:
1. If you are not assertive, you must learn to be.
2. Don't cross the line from being assertive to aggressive.
3. You must ask in business. You must ask for the business from your customers. You must ask your customers to pay you.
4. You must say no in business.
5. You cannot be afraid to say no to your employees, your customers or your suppliers.
6. Without follow-up there will not be success.
7. You must follow up with your employees, customers and suppliers.

Chapter 12
Commitment:
Business and family

A new business is as demanding as a marriage. A new business is not a hobby nor an activity you play at. If you are starting something as a supplement to your income, that is one thing. But if you are creating a business to support your family, anything less than a full commitment of your energy and time won't work. Don't believe the advertisements promoting entrepreneurship as an instant leisure lifestyle with loads of money and free time. If you do, you will be disappointed. It is difficult to build a full-time business with part-time effort. Only after your company is a success can you cut back on your effort—not when you start out.

With 80 percent of all new business ventures failing, anything less than your complete dedication and commitment won't do. Dreamers make the mistake of thinking they can start a successful business part time with little money and a partial commitment. That's wishful thinking. If you can't make the commitment, cancel your plans and save your money.

Just what is a commitment?
I view a commitment to be one of two things: (1) a promise or a pledge to a person(s) or (2) an unrelenting dedication to an

objective or cause. Starting a business is such a commitment; it demands that everything be secondary to its success. If you want it to survive, you will focus on it and do little else. It means you must be tenacious—not quitting when problems appear and discourage you.

As with everyone else in business, you will have your share of problems. There will be moments when everything seems to be going wrong. If at times you feel overwhelmed by your problems and are tempted to quit, don't. These are the moments to remain steadfast. If you wish you were at your old job, be careful; the past can be misleading. Instead, remember why you started your business.

I think of such situations as the testing and preparation phase for prosperity. If you quit when times are tough, two things will happen: (1) you will lose your money, and (2) you will never know that if you had tried a little longer, you may have succeeded. A common cause of business failure is quitting too soon.

To quit a business is a tough decision to make. Some people will advise you to cut your losses, get out and go back to your old job. Others will advise the opposite. It is easy to find yourself in a situation of not knowing what to do. Your indecisiveness can be an emotionally draining experience—particularly so if you are deep in debt and you need more money to keep your business open. It can be tempting to shut it down before it takes everything you have.

Granted, it is difficult to know how long you should stay and fight, but unless your doors are closed by creditors or the Internal Revenue Service, it is still your decision whether to stay in business. Regardless of how much money you have invested, it is actually lost only when you permanently close the business.

While each situation is different, if you can keep your doors open, without putting more personal funds in the business or personal guarantees, do so. As long as the business is alive, there is the possibility of survival. And there is no stronger will than the will to survive.

It's a family affair

The first year of the new business can be emotional for an entrepreneur's family. There probably will be worries over money and the survival of the firm. Because of these strains, family cohesiveness and mutual support and understanding are essential. If there are disagreements over goals, participation or the need to sacrifice, the chance of success may be slim. Without a unity of purpose by family members, it will be difficult to get through the challenging start-up phase. Family support and teamwork are essential for success.

If you are married, it needs to be a solid one. Troubled relationships add a dangerous dimension that can kill a new business. If you frequently fight, have disagreements over lifestyles or family money problems, how can you concentrate on your goals? Marital problems can be distracting and discouraging. They can drain you of your optimism and energy which are so vital to your new venture. If you are experiencing such difficulty, don't start a business until you have resolved your problems and have a clear understanding of your common goals and lifestyle requirements.

A new business can place a lot of pressure on any marital relationship. The entrepreneur of the family will need to remain focused on just one thing: the success of the business. The family conversation will probably be about the business to such an extent it will become repetitious. Without question, it will dominate all aspects of the relationship. Be prepared for the excitement and the challenge of it to crowd out everything else for a while. It will definitely test the bonds of your marriage.

Before making the investment and quitting your job, be sure you have an understanding with your spouse of all that a new venture demands. Both of you must understand the risk and sacrifice that will be necessary. If either is fantasizing about immediate wealth, watch out; there will be disappointment.

Let me share with you the story of Ken and Mary, who started a small combination retail and wholesale electronics company. For a while, they appeared to be doing well, but each had a different view of the business. Ken was always in a hurry to expand and seemed unaware of the money problems. Mary was conservative and worried a lot. Whenever she managed to have the bills under control, Ken bought more inventory and told her to stop worrying as he knew best. With too much unsold merchandise and too many bills, they slid into bankruptcy. It was an unnecessary failure that could have been prevented if they had developed mutual goals.

A business plan is more than numbers

A business plan can play a vital role in reaching a common ground of understanding by a couple or family. If the plan is written and understood by all concerned, there should be no surprises to anyone. If, however, your level of expectation is too high, there may be disappointment. Set your goals high, but keep your expectations reasonable. Success takes twice as long to happen than we imagine.

I know of a young couple that went into business without a business plan and little understanding of what it takes to get established. They were accustomed to instant gratification and unwilling to postpone pleasure. Before long, one spouse grew tired of waiting and began demanding a prosperous lifestyle including a European vacation. The argument to enjoy life was: "I deserve it!"

They were unprepared for the sacrifice that the struggling small business demanded. Apparently, it was a good marriage only during good times; they split when the business failed.

If you are married and about to start a business, share your business plan with your spouse and if possible, develop it together. With a mutual understanding of the expected problems and the potential for failure, you will be a better team. Teamwork and trust can make the difference between failure and success. Working at cross purposes is self-defeating and costly.

A business plan can be helpful in establishing common goals. It helps you stay more focused and not be distracted by diverse wants and needs. Sharing your business plan as well as mood swings of optimism and pessimism with your spouse or another best friend can also be a stabilizing influence.

Divorce is deadly
Divorce can cause business failure. With nearly half of all marriages ending in divorce, I'm surprised it is not often cited as a

major cause of business bankruptcy. Just as divorce can destroy a family's financial security, it can bankrupt a business. If the business is one that both spouses struggled and sacrificed to develop, there probably will be a conflict in the divorce proceedings over the business assets or even the ownership and control of the business.

Even if one spouse wishes to buy out the other, how is a fair price determined by two warring parties? Plus, it may be difficult to get any agreement if there is bitterness and distrust. Then there is the problem of getting the money to complete the buyout. Does one borrow or attempt to sell off a piece of the business? If borrowing is a possibility, can the business handle the debt? These are just some of the questions and problems that a divorce can create.

During the divorce proceedings, the business will suffer in many other ways. There will an absence of direction and leadership as the couple is preoccupied with their problems. There will be uncertainty over the future of the business. Creditors and employees may become nervous. Customers may speculate. The morale and motivation of everyone associated with the business will be affected. Unfortunately, the more difficult the divorce and the longer the proceedings are dragged out, the more likely the business will fold.

Let me tell you the sad tale of one middle-aged couple that lost a very profitable business because of a ruined marriage and an ugly divorce. Their story began when after months of searching throughout New England, they found a neglected delicatessen in a small New Hampshire town near the White Mountains at a price they could afford. By working 16-hour days and saving every possible dollar, they managed to make a success of it. As they prospered, they added to their business with a second location, followed by a small restaurant and a beauty parlor.

By all appearances, it looked as if they were well on their way to success—he drove a new Corvette and she decorated their new home. As a couple they worked hard and were a presence in the community.

But for whatever reason, the husband began an illicit romance with an employee and the affair was discovered by his wife. The ensuing separation and divorce proceedings were bitter. Following the separation, the husband continued his relationship with the employee. Everyone in the town was aware of the situation and many customers boycotted the deli and restaurant.

Eventually, due to money problems, the restaurant and the beauty parlor were closed and the second deli was sold. What had been a prosperous group of enterprises was reduced to a faltering, nearly empty deli—all due to disloyalty followed by divorce.

The deli was taken over by new investors and is doing very well. Our ill-fated entrepreneur is living with his girlfriend and pumping gas.

I know of another case where a couple built a very successful dry cleaning business and lost it all over a divorce. When the business was flourishing, the husband began taking frequent afternoons off to play golf, or so he said, while his wife continued to dedicate herself to the business.

When the husband's adulterous activities were discovered, he became arrogant and assumed he could manage the business without his wife. She, being a fighter, demanded her fair share and was in no hurry to settle for anything less. Finally, their lawyers advised them to settle and not go into court because it might trigger an Internal Revenue Service investigation. They settled and closed the business.

It was a very costly affair. She now lives on Social Security. He remarried and continues working even though he is old enough to retire. There is still bitterness over the affair and the needless loss of everything.

If you are bent on self-destruction, start a new business with a troubled marriage or taste a little success and screw up your marriage. In either case you can add a business failure to your resume.

Remember:
1. A new business is like a marriage—your total commitment is required.
2. A new business is not a hobby.
3. A new business will dominate all of your life and test your patience and fortitude.
4. A common cause of business failure is quitting too soon.
5. Family support and commitment are critical for success.
6. A shaky marriage spells disaster when starting a new business.
7. A business plan is a big help in establishing a family under standing of the business and its challenges.
8. Divorce can bankrupt you and your business.

PART FOUR
Applying successful sales and marketing strategies

If you have any fear about selling, get over it. If your new business is going to survive, learn to sell your product or service without hesitating to ask for the order. As you will read in the next few chapters, most successful sales, marketing and promotional activities are based on the premise of "asking for the order." As master salesman Red Motley said, "Nothing happens until someone sells something."

Ask yourself: "Am I sales minded?" It can affect your attitude. Don't fall for the myth that sales persons are born not made. Sales training and motivation can be learned and are essential to your business's survival.

Chapter 13
Promotion:
Don't hide your business

If you think promotion is obvious, let me tell you about Frank. Already the owner of a large and successful auto parts manufacturing company in Detroit, Frank started a plastic injection molding company to produce small parts for the auto industry.

As he hoped, he was able to persuade one of the "Big Three" to do business with his new plastics company. He was lucky; it was profitable from the start. His one customer placed so many orders for a series of plastic knobs for switches and controls that the plant was required to operate two shifts, five days a week. By the end of the first year he landed a second customer.

Although the entire business rested on the orders of two customers, it did not concern him. As his plant was operating at near capacity, Frank felt no need for any sales or promotional activity. He did not see the need for any catalog material, price sheets or merchandising aids. He did print business cards for himself and hung a small sign on the front of the building.

Aware of the risk of depending on two customers, his manager suggested they hire a sales person to develop new customers.

Frank disagreed. He viewed most sales and promotional activities as unnecessary expenses. After all, he told his manager, was he not running two shifts and earning a profit?

His immediate success fostered a sense of false security. His first company had survived for years working for the major auto companies. He had no reason to think differently about his plastics plant.

Then one day, after three years of success, his business dropped off sharply. The company went from $200,000 a month in sales to $25,000. With so much of his customers' final assembly now in Mexico and elsewhere, molding plastic parts in Michigan became impractical.

Frank took drastic action. He ordered his operations manager to lay off most of the work force and operate on a single half-shift schedule; yet, the company still lost money—so much so that Frank debated the possibility of shutting the company's doors and leaving the plastics industry. But liquidating the business meant losing most of his investment; he was not prepared to do so. Over the next few months, the losses ate up all the profits from the good years. He knew the business could continue to exist only if his other company helped pay the bills.

To keep the business alive, it meant starting over as no one in the plastics industry, except for suppliers, was aware of the company. The total absence of promotional and marketing activity was evident.

Although stubborn, Frank was also lucky. After a year of sales and promotional efforts by Frank and his manager, the company obtained work molding plastic cases for a few cosmetics and drug companies.

Frank learned his lesson. The company now works with a local advertising and promotion agency and employs a full-time sales person.

Awareness of your business

Potential customers need to know you exist—a basic awareness of your business. Before you open your doors you should have an understanding of whom your customers are, where your customers are and how many you can sell to. Customers need to be able to find you. And customers need to remember you. Don't assume a single ad, a single article, your business card, a small sign or a listing in the yellow pages will do it for you. It won't.

Nearly everyone worldwide knows Coca-Cola®, yet the company spends millions each year on advertising and promotion. Why? To protect their market. They know that customers forget, that customers are tantalized by competitors and that customers like to buy what they know.

There are many market studies concluding consumers don't like change. There is evidence that consumers are more reluctant to change than they are willing to admit. If this is so, how do new products and brands succeed? They succeed through sufficient promotion to take the edge off the newness. It is a paradox; we want new products and services, but we want someone else to try them first.

As you plan for your company's future, a public relations/

promotion strategy may be as important as a financial strategy. But remember, awareness takes time. It does not happen quickly. It requires a credible message repeated many times.

You can't expect to do any business if no one knows you are in business. It is foolhardy to think the market will search you out. Whatever your market, your potential customers must know your business exists if they are to do business with you. Even if you have built the proverbial "better mouse trap," if no one knows about it, how can they buy it? The market must discover your business now.

Calling attention to yourself is "promoting" the awareness of your business. The more competitors you have, the more important it is to lay out a public relations and promotion plan. Sports and entertainment celebrities are paid millions to endorse companies and their products. Why? Public recognition and association help promote awareness, which leads to sales.

Appearance

If you recall, Chapter 10 stressed the importance of good house-keeping to the success of your new business. Just as your company's physical appearance is a statement about how you manage your business, your communications and promotional messages also create the image of your company.

For example, if you see a hand-lettered cardboard sign tacked to a tree along the highway advertising produce or pets for sale, does it make you want to stop? I doubt it. Cardboard signs are temporary; perhaps the business is too—not a very positive image.

Right or wrong, we judge people by the way they look; we formulate our initial opinions from their appearance. Your potential customers will do the same regarding your business. Your promotional and advertising messages will attract or repel. If a potential customer does not know you or your business, what you say about your firm may decide whether that person wishes to be your customer.

Your initial image

As you develop your business, the image you create can attract, discourage or intimidate customers. Your image can be "down to earth," it can be snooty, it can radiate caring and quality, it can be family value oriented or it can be sleazy. It can be whatever you wish it to be. The time to decide your image is when you start the business. Undoing a negative or incorrect image is costly and time consuming. In addition, consumer complaints, quality complaints and questionable practices can all result in negative promotion.

Employees

Employees with attitude problems send strong negative messages. Customers do not like to do business with employees who are not courteous, knowledgeable and helpful. Incompetent or rude employees can cause you to lose customers, even your business. Employees are part of your public relations activity. It is not only your sales people who have contact with the public; sooner or later, every employee will in some manner.

Have you ever attempted to hire a plumber, electrician or carpenter only to have them not return your phone calls or fail to show up for appointments without notifying you? What was your impression?

Employees who fail to return phone calls, fail to follow up with promises made to customers or fail to keep appointments are a liability to you. Such attitudes and actions can be costly. Don't tolerate it. Disgruntled workers can do your new business serious harm. Firing them is cheaper.

Happy, productive employees are wonderful advertisements. By word of mouth they can create goodwill with prospective employees, the community and customers.

Community relations

If your business is in a community of modest size, your actions may be under a microscope. The public, which may include your customers and employees, can quickly formulate an opinion of your business. Be certain your community views your new venture as a benefit—not a problem to the neighborhood.

There are many things you can do to develop a positive community image. You may become involved in service organizations such as the Lions or Rotary. You may contribute to local popular and worthwhile causes. You may support your schools, hospitals and community recreation activities. If you can afford it, think about establishing a partial scholarship for a deserving youngster in the community.

Positive community relations should be part of the promotional strategy of every business. Don't be shortsighted and think such image-building activity is not important because you don't get any immediate income from it.

Customers

Happy customers can be effective goodwill ambassadors. Their word of mouth endorsements are invaluable and highly credible. On the other hand, as difficult as it may be to please everyone, try to avoid creating dissatisfied customers. While good news travels slowly, customer complaints travel at great speed.

Press releases

A news item about your company and its products or services in the local paper or a trade magazine can be beneficial. A news story, such as a move to larger quarters, a new product, the promotion of an employee or a research breakthrough, may be seen as a sign of success and progress. Everyone knows an advertisement is a paid message with a built-in bias, but a news item is assumed to be objective. While customers may question the claims of an advertisement, they will most readily accept a news article at face value.

If your industry has a trade publication and most do, subscribe to it. If you have a new product or service, send an article with photos about it to the editor. If you land a major contract or customer, send a press release to the editor. Trade publications are always looking for news. No, you don't have to advertise to get your material published. There is no quicker way to develop recognition, outside of an expensive advertising campaign, than a series of well-written, well-placed news articles.

If your industry has various directories, make sure your company is listed. Get your company listed in every related or applicable directory you can find.

At times the business section of the local newspaper may do stories on business firms. Call the editor and see if there is any interest in a story about your new business.

If writing is not something you do well, there are plenty of freelance writers looking for extra money. Check with any college offering a program in journalism; they will be able to help you.

You will find it rewarding to see news about the success of your company in the press. The right material can quickly establish your company in the minds of the market, the industry and the public. And outside of the fee to a writer, it's free!

The right image
I think the ideal image is a combination of positive images.

When you start your business it is important that you cultivate the image of "staying power"—not that of a fly-by-night operator entering the market with a flashy splash, only to disappear shortly, leaving unpaid bills. If customers and creditors think you won't be around for the long haul, they will avoid you. Your new customers and creditors must be comfortable with you. They must believe in your success—your staying power.

Look at the leading competitors in your industry. What image of longevity do they create? Study it. Adapt it to your needs. Study their promotional material, their press releases; look at how they package their product and services. Don't worry about losing your individuality; emulate the style of their success, not the details of it. Look at the image activity of the losers; if you see anything that reminds you of your company, change it.

Work to establish the image that you care about your customers, appreciate their business and value them as customers. Remember, the idea of caring about your customer begins with caring about the quality of your product or service. If you want to stay in business, make caring a main part of your image and your business practices.

Honesty is a virtue successful companies endorse. Businesses that engage in dishonest practices are in time discovered. I am not aware of significant long-term successful companies that are dishonest in most dealings. Crooked companies don't last. Suppliers stop dealing with them. Customers go elsewhere. And the Internal Revenue Service, sooner or later, will pay a visit.

Remember:

1. To do business, people must know you are in business.
2. Calling attention to your business is promoting the awareness of your business.
3. A public relations and promotion strategy may be as important as a financial strategy.
4. Your communications messages help create the image of your company.
5. The time to think about your image is when you start your business.
6. Employees are an important part of your image.
7. Make sure your community sees your business as a benefit not a problem.
8. Happy customers are valuable to your image.
9. The right image consists of staying power, caring and honesty.

Chapter 14
Market research:
Finding and understanding
your customers

You may feel you know your business will succeed. You may feel you know that your product or service will sell. Yet, feelings and reality can be quite different. As you plan your business, be cautious of wishful thinking replacing insight and facts. Wishful thinking can prove disastrous. Before you commit your money and yourself to your venture, you must have answers to the questions: (1) Who are my customers?, (2) Where are they?, (3) How many are there?, (4) Will they buy from me? and (5) How much will they buy from me?

If you must guess or have little knowledge of the answers you may be fooling yourself with wishful thinking. Even major corporations make costly blunders because they do not check out the market. Remember the "New Coke." Just as most new businesses fail, so do most new products. Much of the new business failure rate is caused by the lack of knowledge about customers. Acting hastily and on hunches can result in wrong decisions.

Market research is good insurance. It is essential research that replaces wishful thinking with facts. It is in keeping with the adage "forewarned is forearmed." It is wonderful to find out good news from your market research that your product, service or whatever is going to be a winner and you are going to "knock the socks off your competition." However, do not hide from the bad news and pretend it does not exist—wishful thinking can put you out of business.

What do you really need to know?

Market research can be costly and complex or it can be simple research that requires no special training or background. The amount and type of research will depend on what you need to know to make an informed and objective decision. As you will find out, information can be expensive. Do not rush out and contract with a market research firm just to feel safe. Limit your inquiry to a need-to-know basis. In other words, how much must you know to reasonably answer the questions who, where, how many, will they and how much will they buy? Overkill is just as big a mistake as too little information. I know from a first-hand experience.

Let me tell you about an embarrassing moment in my career. In 1960, fresh with my MBA from Boston University, I joined the management planning staff of Capitol Records in Hollywood.

At that time Capitol Records manufactured and distributed a line of phonographs, including home console models, to its various record dealers. Because of lackluster sales, however, the company decided to discontinue manufacturing and shrink the model line to a few portables to be manufactured by a subcontractor. I was given the assignment of preparing a market research report on the potential of the new portable line. I was excited with the assignment as here was a chance to demonstrate my talents for all of management to see.

A month later, on a Friday afternoon, I handed the director of Management Planning a 100-page report loaded with charts, graphs and the most recent consumer electronics and phonograph market statistics. I believed it to be a wealth of information.

As I was impressed with my handiwork, I expected to get a call over the weekend telling me what a great job I had done. But I did not. On Monday there was no mention of the report. By the end of the week, I could not contain myself any longer; I asked the director if he had any comments about it. He said he did not at the moment, but that he would discuss it with me in a few days. As you may imagine, my inflated ego was bruised.

The following Monday he called me into his office and explained that although my report was very complete and detailed, it did not address the problem. All he wanted to know was approximately how many of our record dealers would handle the product line and approximately how many units could they anticipate selling during the season. He was not concerned about the size and growth of the entire consumer electronics industry. In the interim, he had given the assignment to another staff member for a "quick" look at the situation.

I missed the mark. I applied an academic research approach to a simple request for data and I committed overkill. It was an important lesson to me. My conversion to brevity and simplicity was immediate.

Balance the cost of data with the risk

Information is expensive. It takes time to gather and the research hours can be costly. When you need to know something about market potential or your customers, ask yourself: How much money am I putting at risk? How important are the answers to my questions? Will the information really make a difference in my decision? Will the answers to my questions matter?

If the future of your business is going to hinge on a new product, a unique marketing strategy or advertising campaign, check your facts before committing yourself. The more important the action to your success, the less the margin of error you can afford to have and the more information you may need.

Big companies with ample cash or credit can make big blunders and survive. Can you? Just as you do not take unnecessary risks because you assume you know the facts, do not delay or procrastinate making a decision because you do not know every possible detail. Strike a happy medium. Work to balance your risk with the cost and time of the research necessary to make the decision.

Customers: Who are they? Where are they? How many are there?

Unless you have a background with the product or market, it is a mistake to think you automatically know who your customers are, where they are and how many. You must reach the right market to succeed. If you think this information is unimportant or you are too busy for find out about your market, then you could be courting failure.

Who are they?

Before starting to sell your product or service it is wise to identify possible customers. Without such information, how else can
you develop the best marketing approach or appeal?

Can you visualize what your average customer is like? Are they
other business firms? Are they government agencies or institutions? Are they consumers? If so, what are their ages? Are they
married? What are their interests and/or hobbies? What education levels do they have? What profession or occupation is most
common? Are religious or political ties important? What habits
do they have? What is their profession or vocation? How do
they spend their money? What do they want from life? Are they
young or old? Are they single or married and is it important?
Do they have children?

These are the basic questions. While you may not have all the
answers, this information should help you define your customer
base, which in turn will help you plan any advertising or promotions. You may find it helpful to create a profile (in your
mind or better yet, on paper) of how you perceive your average
customer. Develop an understanding of that profile and compare it to any research you do. Attempting to appeal to the
wrong market or customers will not work!

As you develop your product or your service, plan your location
or create the theme of your business, the image or profile of
your average customer must influence your plans. As I missed
the mark with my report, you cannot afford to miss the mark
with your business. The key is knowing your customer better
than yourself. All that you do in creating your business must be
done with your customer in mind.

To repeat myself, one reason for business and product failure is not understanding who the customers are. Do not rush into business without finding out about whom you expect to buy your product or services. Ignorance can be fatal.

Where are they?
Even if you know who they are, you should know where they are. If you do not, how are you going to contact them? Do they live in a specific area or city? Are they city-dwellers, suburbanites or rural residents? Are they clustered or widespread? Are they local, regional, national or international?

The major fast food chains spend substantial research dollars to determine the right locations for their outlets. They know they need to go to where their customers are. Major retailers of all types understand the importance of location. Look at the depressing "downtown" shopping areas in many of our cities. The retailers followed the population to the suburbs. Now many of our neighbors are leaving the suburbs for rural areas, with new stores right behind them.

"Where are they" means understanding customer habits so you can reach them through newspapers, magazines and any special interest publications. When do they read? Do they bother with local papers and "throwaways?" Do they pay attention to circulars and posters? What is their opinion of "occupant" mail? Which radio and TV programs do they like? When do they listen to the radio or watch TV? Do they "live" on the Internet, spending many hours a day online?

How many are there?

How big is your market? Will it support your new business? Estimating the size of a market can be a very difficult task. Unfortunately, the answers may be no more than educated guesses. If your product or service is new and unique, forecasting the demand with accuracy may be near impossible. Your hunch may be right; however, if at all possible, attempt to verify it. Be cautious of too much reliance on "feelings."

There are a variety of methods you may use to estimate a potential market, some quite sophisticated others simple (later in this chapter I explain some simple approaches). Beyond my treatment of the subject in this book, you may wish to investigate some of the basic approaches contained in most market research textbooks.

If after your research you find the estimate of your market is smaller than your original projections, rethink your plans if you can. Do not base your expenses and overhead on a market that will not support your business. Plan your business in relation to the size of your most immediate, potential market. Long-term forecasts and plans are fine, but you will need short-term success to stay in business.

If you forecast, it is wiser to err on the conservative side. If you forecast sales too high, you will have a surplus of inventory that may put you out of business. Distress sales are not profitable. If you understate your forecast, the worst problem you face will be that of a shortage and some impatient customers—troublesome, but not fatal.

Why they buy what they do

It is not enough to know who, where and how many. If you want customers to buy your product or service, you must know why they buy what they do. What motivates their buying decisions? Is it price, quality, status, fear, service, security or some other reason that triggers a positive buying decision?

Is there a prime motivating force you can tap? I think you must know about it to successfully appeal to it. Some claim we are all selfish to a certain extent and that we are moved by appeals to our selfish motives. J.P. Morgan once proved that you can motivate nearly anyone if you find their "hot button." His nephew, who was away at college, would never answer letters from his family. Mr. Morgan wrote a letter stating: "Enclosed is a ten dollar bill." But he purposefully omitted the money. Within days, he received a letter back from his nephew, telling him that the ten dollars was not in the envelope.

The motivating forces that cause customers to buy a product are not always visible. Some are quite complex, some are subconscious and some we prefer not to admit. Advertising professionals schooled in psychology and consumer behavior know how to tap our inner-psyche to spur us to action. They know how to appeal to our fear of disaster and loss when advertising smoke alarms and fire insurance. They know how to touch our greed with ads for commodity options. They tell us if we change our hair color or use the right after-shave cologne, we will find love and romance. And if we eat the right breakfast cereal, it will bring us health and well-behaved children. Any ad or sales message that ignores the conscious or subconscious reasons why customers buy a product or service is not good promotion.

A few research tools

Here are the basic tools to collect market research data in the order you're most likely to use them in your business.

Associations

Almost every industry and type of business activity has some form of a trade association. These associations are usually comprised of similar businesses that make up the membership and provide the association with financial support. These associations may lobby on behalf of their membership as well as provide research and information about the industry and market conditions and trends. Even though you may not be a member, many will provide you with industry and marketing data hoping your company will join. A wealth of information is yours for the asking.

Another valuable source of marketing research is the local chamber of commerce in your city or community. The chamber directory can help you identify local businesses that are potential customers (as well as competitors).

Do you recall the story of Frank and his plastics plant? Well, the prime source of locating manufacturing companies that outsourced their injection molding needs came from the local chamber of commerce. In a very real sense, the information provided by the local chamber of commerce saved his company.

If you need information about associations, go to the reference section of your local library and ask for the "Encyclopedia of Associations." Most associations are listed. Another helpful source of information is the industrial trade directory published for each state. If you live near a college or university library, investigate the reference section. While you may not be able to check materials out, you may be able to browse at length. Local libraries are very useful, too. Also try your local yellow pages, not to mention searching online using the name(s) of your industry(ies) paired with the word "associations."

A few telephone calls
I love firsthand data. I take a somewhat unorthodox approach to market research. I like to play investigative reporter and make a few phone calls.

I recall an instance during the early days of Adams Magnetic Products when we were looking to expand our product catalogue by adding dictation recording cassettes. As we knew little about the competitive climate or the sales potential, I called three of our customers to find out if they sold the items and would they buy from us. Without hesitation I was told at what price we would need to sell the cassettes to be competitive and the approximate quantity they purchased. Considering the responses from our three customers, we successfully added the product.

Why would they tell me such information? Over the years I have found that simply by asking direct questions you will get some very direct answers. People want to be helpful, especially if they stand to benefit from answering the questions. If you take an open and honest approach in seeking information and telling the person why the data is important to you, usually you will get an honest and helpful answer. It pays to ask!

It is amazing what you can learn in a short time. It is simple and may be accurate for your needs. It can give you a quick insight and may tell you if you need more information to make a decision, how to avoid a potential problem or how to pursue a market.

Steve is a sales representative for a few companies in the construction and landscape supply business. He came upon a "unique" contractor's tool manufactured as a sideline by an acquaintance of his. The friend asked Steve to represent him. Steve agreed and began promoting it to tool and hardware distributors as well as selling it to contractors and construction workers. Initially, all seemed well with a rash of orders. But after two months the manufacturer knew there was a problem because he was not getting paid. It turned out that the product was collecting dust on his customers' shelves and not selling. Contractors looked at it and made comments about the price. Few bought it. Eventually the distributors demanded to return the merchandise. The owner of the tool company was given the unpleasant choice of bad debt or a warehouse of "dead" inventory.

Telephone calls to the initial distributors asking how well the tool was selling may have avoided the disaster. The product failed in the market because it was not selling to the end-user. Why? Could it have been resurrected? Maybe, it was certainly worth finding out. If it were my company and my money, I would have been on the telephone. A dozen telephone calls could have done it.

Steve is the culprit in the eyes of the toolmaker. Yet, the real culprit was the entrepreneur as he did no research on pricing, packaging or the best way to distribute the item.

Visit customers and competitors (if you can)

Go to where the action is. If you are selling a product to wholesalers or retailers, visit them. Watch what is happening (if anything) with your merchandise. Observe the consumers or endusers. Are they buying it? What is their reaction to the item? Check with the salesperson(s)—what do they think of your product? If the item is not selling, there is no better way to find out why than being on the scene. It may save your business. There are many top executives who frequently spend a day in the field making surprise visits to retailers who sell their products. From these field trips they are able to develop a first hand "feel" about the market. Not only do they see their product in action, they also see the competition.

If you are in the retail business, visit your competition. A few moments in their store(s) will tell you a great deal. You will come away with fresh ideas about competing. Watch and listen. Your powers of observation are important to your survival. Remember, wishful thinking and false assumptions can be costly.

Competitive analysis

To compete successfully you must know your competition. Investigate your competitors' strengths and weaknesses. Go beyond the product and look at your competition's pricing, distribution policies, credit terms, advertising and merchandising. As you probably know, there are few original ideas. Look to the success of your competition for some of your success.

Develop a list of the features and policies (e.g., your warranty) and compare them item by item with your competition's. Once you understand how your product or service stacks up against the competition, you can begin to make the changes necessary to make your business more attractive to your customers in the marketplace.

Surveys and Statistics. Survey results are everywhere today. Politicians read and rely on the latest poll information to measure campaign strengths or weaknesses. Many of their decisions to support or oppose issues may be based on information from the polls. Just as pollsters play a pivotal role in election campaigns, market researchers influence the actions of management in most major corporations. From surveys, management and politicians alike are guided by what is perceived as a reading of the attitudes and wants of the public.

We make extensive use of surveys as a basic research tool. As you know, there are survey results published daily on most any topic. We have come to rely on such information for a variety of decisions. Nevertheless, just as surveys can give us a wealth of information, they can misguide us as well with erroneous or misleading data.

The market (or group) researchers are interested in, such as all the registered voters in an upcoming election, is referred to as the "universe." The portion or number of voters we solicit for information is known as the "sample." If the sample is too small, it may not be accurate. If it is the wrong sample, it may not be accurate. For example, if we are sampling voters and the sample is mostly senior citizens, we may get a distorted view of certain issues. Pollsters and researchers, when publishing their data usually indicate a so-called margin of error. It will usually appear as a footnote: Margin of error plus or minus a certain percentage. A five percent margin of error means the information can be off by 10 percent (five percent too high or five percent too low). Depending on the issue at hand, that could be significant.

Surveys and the use of statistics to explain the results have become a pseudo-science. There are all kinds of sampling techniques in use. The sample can be at random. It could instead be based on any common denominator within the group you are interested in researching, for example, on retail traffic at a certain time of the day, a numerical sequence from the phone book, age, sex or education.

I am reluctant to offer a simple survey plan—the careful preparation of questionnaires is critical to obtain accurate data. Plus, the compilation of the mailing or sample is best left to professionals. Small market research firms can do limited preliminary surveys that may be adequate. Some entrepreneurs can ask for the services of his or her local community college. Most offer marketing courses and such projects are usually welcome.

As an entrepreneur, if you are going to make a decision that can affect your fortunes based on survey results, ask two questions: (1) Was the sample large enough to accurately reflect the total market? and (2) Was the sample a special sample reflecting a unique group within the market?

In my opinion, you should use surveys to guide your decisions, not make them for you. The data should confirm or deny what you think the opportunities are. If you use a survey and you are in disagreement with the results, you may need more information on the subject.

Published Data. Be careful about relying on statistics from government sources. The data may be out of date due to the long lead time in the collection and publication of the material. Although adequate for long-term economic research, the data may not be right for your needs. As mentioned earlier, trade associations and trade publications are additional helpful sources of statistical data. Another helpful source may be your local stockbroker. Major brokerage firms can usually provide all types of industry reports. I also like the Internet and the many web sites for financial data. In fact, while doing any research today, I check the Internet first.

Remember:
1. It can be fatal to assume you know your market.
2. Wishful thinking does not create a market.
3. How much do you need to know? Too little is dangerous. Too much information is costly.
4. You need the answers to the five basic questions about potential customers: Who are they? Where are they? How many are there? Will they buy from you? How much will they buy from you?
5. If you understand what motivates your customers, you will know how to sell to them.
6. Don't overlook your trade association for information.
7. A few phone calls can be revealing—they may save your business.
8. If you can, visit your customers and competitors.
9. Check out your competition. "Know thine enemy."
10. Simple surveys can tell you a lot.

Chapter 15
Advertising:
Asking for the business!

If you remember nothing else in this chapter, please remember that advertising exists only to sell your product or service. It has no other function. That may seem obvious to you but during the 1960s and 70s there were many social critics who questioned the social and productive value of advertising. They said it was a waste of money better spent on social problems. What they failed to appreciate was the true role of advertising—the marketing of products through persuasive information. Again, the only reason to spend money on advertising is to sell your product or service!

Should you advertise? Yes and no!

Here's the "No" answer. If your business is selling to a limited customer base (such as sub-contract manufacturing for a few customers), it may not pay to spend money on any form of media advertising that will reach large groups of readers or viewers. It may be more effective to use a targeted sales campaign directed just to your specific customers or potential customers.

If your customer base is broader, then seriously consider advertising. However, unlike most other products and services you buy, advertising results and benefits are not easy to measure. It is difficult and may even be impossible to apply cost-effective means to advertising. In the beginning of your venture, it is easy to waste money on poor or ineffective advertising. Yet, it is unlikely you will have the money to experiment. There is no right amount to spend on advertising. It depends upon the type of product or service and the size of the business.

Be cautious of advertising "advice." Don't be an explorer or pioneer unless you have deep pockets. Advertising salespersons may know about media costs, frequency of ad discounts and half tones, but do they know anything about your business? Do they know who your customers are, where they are and what to say to them? If not, put your checkbook away.

As you will discover there are many types of advertising media—some good—some not so good. With a limited amount of money to spend promoting your business, deciding on the most beneficial advertising program will not be easy. Just as you shop carefully for your insurance, your equipment and whatever else your business requires, you must be as analytical and critical with every ad dollar you plan to spend. Unlike a product, ads do not carry a warranty and cannot be returned or exchanged.

Target marketing and wasted circulation
"Target marketing" sounds auspicious and important. It is one of those business phrases that had its origins in World War II, such as "tactics" and "strategy." Even if you have never taken a course in management or marketing, don't be put off by such terminology. Target marketing is the result of the questions: Who, Where and How Many? As you may "target" a goal, you must "target" your advertising to the "Who and Where."

Placing ads before readers (or listening or viewing audiences) that will not buy the product is wasting money. In newspaper advertising it is known as "wasted circulation." It is easy to squander your ad budget if you do not pay attention to where your customers are. Ads that are "wasted" on viewers or readers not located in your geographical market is a foolish waste of your money.

Aim correctly. Each message you display, transmit or mail to a potential customer costs you money. Make sure you are sending messages to people who can buy your product or service. Make sure you understand who and where your customers are. Most newspapers and even national magazines publish regional editions to assist advertisers in "targeting" their ads. Most print media companies publish reader profiles and readership statistics. It may be helpful, but be cautious when looking at such data. Its purpose is to sell advertising.

If you are buying radio or television spots, be careful of package deals. Although reasonable, they give you no control over the ad schedule. I know of a restaurant that grabbed at the chance to contract for a block of spots over a summer season at a very reasonable rate. However, the cable company ran the spots as fillers at three and four a.m. The restaurant reached only the insomniac market.

The same restaurant then tried radio with 20-second spots sandwiched between teenage rock-and-roll selections. They got cheap spots but no customers. Shortly thereafter the management of the restaurant soured on advertising as a waste of money. Management never took the time to understand its customers. It just assumed that by advertising in the popular television and radio media it would reach everyone. The restaurant eventually closed and reopened with new management.

Communication has become a complex subject. We hear and see thousands of messages every day, from signs to broadcasts. We have learned to tune out most of them. We respond to what we like and what we want. It is a challenge for anyone to place a message in front of us that we will notice.

Wrong ads in the wrong place make money only for the media, not you. If you want me to notice your ad, then appeal to my self-interest and place your message where I cannot miss it. I will not hunt for it.

Before you start spending your working capital on any type of ad campaign, be cautious, be thoughtful and place yourself in the position of your customer. Remember the customer profile in Chapter 14; identify with it. How do you wish customers to think of your business? It is easy to create a negative image but it is difficult to undo it!

How many local owners do you see appearing in their own local ads? Too many. Are they effective at presenting their company's products or do they want to be "celebrities"? Most local owners and entrepreneurs are not actors and appear amateurish and they should leave selling messages to professionals. Still, if they really want to see themselves on camera, no one can stop them. Certainly no agency or station is going to discourage it. If you feel strongly about appearing in your ads, consider hiring a media coach to make sure you're putting your best face (and voice) forward.

Where to advertise?

There are unlimited choices for advertising. It is easy to be confused. Every merchant of media claims to be right for your business. They all promise results. They will all tell you it is a mistake not to advertise with them. Yet, none will guarantee a result. Except for mail order and television response ads, it is difficult to measure an ad's pull.

Avoid "specialty" advertising offering giveaways such as calendars, pens and money clips. Ask yourself when did your ever buy a product or service because of a name on a pen or key chain? Specialty advertising items are a way of getting your name before potential customers; however, the problem with such items is that you have little control over who will end up with the specialty item. Also, most people pay little attention to the printing on such items. They want to write with the pen, not read it. Most specialty ad items are goodwill offerings not "selling ads."

Direct mail can be profitable if you have the right addresses and customers; otherwise, it can be costly and wasteful. Mailing campaigns can be expensive. The average response for a successful campaign is only around two or three percent. If you mail a thousand pieces, you may expect 20 or 30 responses. That may or may not be profitable, depending on what you are selling and how much you are selling it for. The rule of thumb for most mail order merchants is that the product must cost (not counting the advertisement cost) no more than one-third of the selling price.

Between the cost of printing and postage, it is easy to spend a few dollars per piece of mail. A major mailing can be costly. If the mailing list is inaccurate, out of date or the wrong list, it can be a financial disaster. Major mail order firms, such as Reader's Digest, never market a product by mail unless they do a test mailing and measure the results. Before you embark on a mailing program, test it. Mail a limited number and see what happens; if you receive disappointing results, forget it.

With the growth of cable television, local merchants in many communities are finding television advertising affordable for the first time. There are plenty of local ad production firms that can craft an ad with a reasonable amount of professionalism. In addition, there has developed a re-issue market for previously broadcast (in a different market) professionally prepared ads to be aired locally with a local merchant logo and address. These ads can be effective. They are much better than some with still shots and poor soundtracks you view on many local cable stations.

Size of print ads and placement
Full-page ads in a major publication such as the New York Times are impressive if you can afford it. If your ad budget is substantial and you are a household name or intent on becoming one, perhaps a "big splash" is reasonable. For a start-up business, it is almost always foolish.

Big splashes are iffy
The following two true stories illustrate why you should avoid big splash advertising.

Tony's full-page newspaper ads. Tony, a self-styled real estate developer in my community, lacked any understanding of marketing and promotion. He constructed, with borrowed money, two model homes and went on to announce his plans to the world. He contracted with a local real estate broker (who displayed little understanding of advertising) to promote and sell the development. They ran the usual "open house" with balloons and fanfare and attracted many local "lookers." Tony, whom I suspect was on an ego trip, contracted with a major newspaper with statewide circulation to run a full-page ad for two consecutive Sundays. That was the end of his ad money.

The entire advertising and promotional approach was abysmal. In front of one of the models was a ridiculous looking washtub propping up a sign announcing the hours the model supposedly was open for viewing (which it seldom was). The project fell into financial ruin and Tony went to work as a contractor's helper. With the right approach the project could have been successful. The models were attractive and reasonably priced with wonderful lakeside views. Nevertheless, the mismanagement of the advertising and sales promotion activities killed it.

The development was ideal for retirees looking to spend the summer in the cool Northeast. I suggested to Tony a series of small ads in senior publications and widely distributed retirement real estate brochures, but he rejected my idea. In my opinion it was a reverse approach of selling Florida real estate to Northern snowbirds. One may miss the "one-time" big ad. It is the repetitive aspect of the ads that eventually catches the eye.

Don't be like Tony. Be careful how you spend your advertising dollars. Do not blow them on one or two ads. As any successful advertising executive will tell you, it is important to get your message to as many potential customers as often as you can. Realize that a large, one-page ad or a major, one-time television ad is costly and gives you only one opportunity to get a potential customer's attention. It is like placing all your money on one turn of the cards.

Many small ads can be more effective and cheaper as the next story will soon show. Small frequent ads can send a message of stability. If you can routinely place your business or product before your buying public, name recognition may develop. A big splash is fine for a movie or book that has a short life but not typically for a small business. You will need more than a grand opening to stay in business.

As you will find, name recognition in business develops slowly. You can nurture it with advertising but only if you have ample money to spend on a big advertising campaign spread out over time.

John and his "big" yellow page ad. Shortly after John opened his store, a representative from the local phone company convinced him of the importance of establishing a presence in the yellow pages with a full-page ad. After all, the salesperson stressed to John, a new business must stand out above the competition. John agreed. As a business major in college, he studied advertising and believed in it.

Unfortunately, the business did not do well the first year and cash became short. As the cost of the ad was part of the monthly telephone bill, he had no choice but to pay it on time. When he could not, the telephone was shut off. No, the telephone company was not flexible.

With help, John survived his start-up cash crisis and has successfully grown his business. He now places a small ad in the yellow pages that he finds is just as effective as his expensive full-page ad.

Placement or position

The location or position of the ad in a publication is as important as the selection of the publication. It must be visible to your public. In magazines, the inside front cover, the center spread and the inside and outside back cover are the most desirable locations and the most costly. Frequent large advertisers reserve these spots months in advance.

With most publications you will have a variety of options as to where to place your ad. With certain products and services there are traditional publications and spots in the publication. For example, in the sports section of the your morning paper, you will find auto repair ads aimed at the male market. In the book review section or supplement, you will find book ads. If your business's market is not that identifiable, follow your successful competitor's approach. Don't be afraid of competition. Welcome it—there are few successful shopping centers with only one store.

Over the years, advertising researchers have done numerous studies on the most retentive positions for print ads. In my opinion, from experience and study, small ads (1/4- or 1/8-page) are most effective, positioned in the upper outside corner, while the lower inside corner is the least productive as the ad is easily overlooked.

The advertising phrase, "a buried ad," refers to a poorly-placed ad that the majority of readers never see. As you become aware of advertising from an entrepreneur's view, you will become aware of how poorly-placed ads are a waste of money.

The basics of a good ad

Do you remember Nissan and the "Enjoy the ride" campaign? The advertising world loved it for its creativity and originality. Yet, it was a failure. Sales dropped 30% and heads rolled. Why? The sales message was passive. Toys and dolls did not offer reasons to buy. The campaign was wonderful entertainment, but weak on any rationale to spend thousands on a new car. Beware of the creative artists and writers at ad agencies who view advertising mostly as an artistic statement, not as a marketing vehicle.

A truly successful ad sells. To do so there are certain basic ingredients the ad must contain.

What do you want to say?

Be clear and certain of what you wish to say. Formulate an answer to the question: Why should anyone buy my product or service? A complex answer will be confusing. And a rambling or too generalized answer will not be convincing. Keep your message simple and clear. Since you are paying for every word, use the right ones. Test your ads. Rough out your ad message and ask some of your customers for their thoughts. Create your own free of charge focus group. It may be surprising what you will find. Listening to your customers may save you from making costly mistakes.

I have a pet peeve with some of my fellow professors. Many have little understanding of the importance of clear and concise writing. What good is a message if no one understands it? If you are having a problem explaining in simple terms what your business is all about and why people should do business with you, ask your customers; they can tell you. Ask: "Why do you do business with my company?" You will surprise them with your approach and you will be surprised by their answers.

Beware of yelling at the audience, a creative technique I find offensive. Not a very intelligent tactic! It does not say much for your message if you must yell to obtain attention. All the media (broadcast or print) contain poor examples of such advertising, from the outlandish claims of car dealers to the use of animated violence to sell toys. Do not confuse originality with effective marketing and selling techniques.

Attention, Interest, Desire and Action (AIDA)

The foundation of every successful advertising and selling campaign rests with the AIDA formula. Your ad must get the reader's or listener's attention. The ad must hold their attention and get their interest. The ad must move the reader, listener or viewer from interest to desire. Finally, you prompt the sale with an action command.

While each of these four steps is in every successful ad, they may not be apparent. A headline, a striking photo or a particular spokesperson may be the attention-getting mechanism. Getting attention is the easiest part of the process. I have demonstrated to my students in my marketing classes that I could always get their attention by kicking a wastebasket across the room. It never failed to raise a few heads. Then I would point out that holding their attention was another matter.

Whatever means you use, it is only a start. Attention is fleeting. The message must be interesting or you will lose the reader or viewer. Effective ads quickly move the person from attention to interest. They use various techniques such as curiosity, offering a bargain, appealing to greed, making a last-time-ever offer and so on. When a potential customer wants to see more, hear more or read more, you are moving him or her to the desire stage. A further explanation of benefits to the prospect may accomplish this. It may be a reinforcement of the conditions that sparked the initial interest. To get action you need an action statement, a command such as: "Call Now," "Order Today," "Valid While Supplies Last," "Act Now," "Don't Delay" and "Limited Offer."

Whatever ad medium you are going to use, the AIDA foundation must be present if your ad is to sell your product. You can get lucky and have a poor ad do well for you and supposedly dispute the experts. By why take the chance? How do you know a good ad? Successful mail order or television response ads are run and rerun. Ineffective ads are cancelled. They do not work.

Other hints

Don't be your own ad agency. Just as you do not attempt to be your own tax accountant or lawyer, don't be your own ad director. Small local agencies can be helpful to your success. You know your product and market. Let the right agency package your message.

If you are selling or distributing product for a company, ask them for advertising materials. Most have professionally prepared advertisements (of various column sizes) ready for any newspaper or magazine. All you need to do is have your agency insert your name and address. You can also arrange for videos of television ads as well as radio scripts for your local AM or FM station.

If you are advertising in trade magazines, reader response cards are wonderful. The publishers of these magazines will mail you a list of all the readers that circle the number of your ad. If your ads are not pulling, you will know it.

If you are going to run classified ads in newspapers or magazines, spend the extra money to block or border them for recognition. Ads, like products on the shelf in a supermarket, need to be visible. Strive for instant awareness. Test it yourself. Scan a newspaper or magazine page: What attracts you? Where is your natural eye movement on the page?

Lastly, here are a few hints about television advertising that may help you. If you are going to do television ads, get professional help. The use of stills with the right soundtrack can be effective. Close-ups are more effective than distance shots. Is your building really that important? Forget family portraits. Interest your customers in what you can do for them, not in your family. Please, do not get out your video camera and decide to become ad director of the year. You will waste your money and perhaps even hurt your image.

Finally, when should you not advertise? If your business is selling to a limited customer base such as subcontract manufacturing for a few clients, it may not pay to spend money on any form of media advertising that will reach large groups of readers or viewers. It may be more effective to use a targeted sales campaign. If your business is a professional practice such as market research or accounting, public relations activities, including an active role in your local chamber of commerce, may be more cost effective than advertising.

Remember:
1. Advertising is not entertainment.
2. Your advertisements must ask for the order.
3. Target your advertising messages; make sure you understand who and where your market is.
4. Be cautious about specialty advertising—most are only for goodwill at best.
5. Do not make a splash-it will not last.
6. Answer the question: Why should someone buy the product from you?
7. Remember the basics of AIDA in all your ads.
8. Keep your ad messages simple and understandable.
9. Don't be your own ad agency.
10. Ask your supplier for available advertising materials— don't reinvent the wheel.

Chapter 16
The art of selling

The very first time Peter went with his sales manager on a sales call he broke out in a rash. During the presentation, whenever his manager turned the sales pitch over to him, he fumbled for words, trying to remember the canned presentation he was required to memorize. The next day he quit, ending his sales career.

During the summer of his junior year, Albert, a marketing major, hoped to gain sales experience. He took a straight commission job selling home improvements to the elderly in lower income neighborhoods. His sales training consisted of memorizing a prewritten presentation based on the fear of fire and theft. He was to be aggressive, to intimidate and to make the sale regardless of need or the ability to pay. Albert hated it. The deceit and dishonesty were not for him. That fall, he changed his major.

These are two typical experiences that can turn off most anybody to selling. Unfortunately, it is a common impression many have. This limited view is based on misunderstandings: that salespeople are dishonest and unethical; that salespeople customarily lie and pressure people into buying, regardless of need or affordability; that selling is based on personality; that sales-people are interested only in their commissions, not the cus-tomer. If you share these misunderstandings, you will have to change your opinion if you are going to succeed in business.

Debunking the myth that you don't have to sell

As you will find out, selling is an integral part of any business activity. If you are already in business, you know it. If you are just starting out, much of your success will depend on your sales skills. If you dislike selling or are fearful of it, read this chapter carefully. It can help you.

In reality, selling is persuading others to your viewpoint, noth-ing more. There is no mystery to it, only hard work and a lot of rejection. Just think of selling as successfully asking someone to do something. It can be learned. It is a skill that comes from practice and positive thinking. If your product or service is competitive and you believe in its value, you can sell it.

The business world is full of successful salespersons who over-came their doubts about selling. If you are uncomfortable about phoning or seeing a stranger to ask for business, you are not alone; nearly every well-known actor has experienced the same discomfort from stage fright. People who must learn public speaking know all about sweaty palms and nervous stomachs. It is only through repeated attempts at selling, acting and speaking do the discomforts begin to vanish—and they will.

As an entrepreneur, you begin your sales career the moment you give birth to the idea of your company. You need to sell your idea to your spouse, your sources of money, your suppliers, your landlord and your new employees. You may not call it selling, but that is what it is. You have a message and you want others to buy it. In your enthusiasm, you do not question your sales ability. You just do it.

Some argue that selling skills are mostly a product of personality. Yes, there is validity to the argument that outgoing people have an easier time of it than shy ones. But whether you are outgoing or quiet, if you have the right message and believe in it, you will persuade others. In my opinion, salesmanship is not based on personality, it is a learned skill, combined with a logical and honest message about a product or service that a potential customer needs or wants. It is nothing more. It is not showmanship or magic. It is the presentation of information in a persuasive manner.

Rejection: Learn to like it

Rejection is a way of life for salespeople. Why? Not every prospect needs a product, nor can everyone afford it. But no one likes to be told no. No one likes rejection regardless of the reason. Some take it personally—some get hurt from the rejection. Why does rejection hurt? Perhaps, because people are too quick to fault themselves with feelings of failure and personal rejection. In business, it is inappropriate to do so.

Your selling and business success will depend on convincing others that you are right. You have the right idea for a business, the right product or right service and you are the right person or firm to deal with. It is not reasonable to think everyone you contact is going to agree with you. Those who say no are not attacking you in a personal sense, but are saying no to your offer—nothing else.

Let me share some sales statistics of rejection with you. If you make 10 sales presentations, regardless of product or service, you may average one sale. That is nine rejections. A 90 percent failure rate. Does that make you a failure? No! It means that 90 percent of the people you approached were not convinced, did not have a need or could not afford your offer. Nothing more!

Remember the chapter on assertiveness and asking—never be afraid or even hesitant to ask for customers, business or money. If fear of rejection is a personal problem for you, see a therapist or start your own self-help program by beginning with small, nonthreatening requests. Getting over the fear of rejection is much like getting over the fear of public speaking. You do it with practice. Rejection is a necessary companion to success. Don't let it hurt and stop you.

A reason to buy

Before you can sell a product or service, you must understand the reason(s) why anyone will buy it. A fundamental of good selling is to discover customer motivation. A sale that requires the benefit of the product must appeal to the self-interest of the prospect. Selling is not exploitation but an act that benefits buyer and seller. To be successful at selling, be prepared; you must know your product or service.

The foundation of your sales presentation is the knowledge of specific reasons why potential customers should buy your product or service. I remember a sales manager who began his sales training sessions by asking his trainees to list 10 specific and objective reasons why a prospect should buy. He insisted on answers with depth. He would not accept generalities such as "our quality is better" or "our product is superior." He demanded specific reasons. He was adamant that his salesforce be knowledgeable about the company and its products. It was his opinion that an informed salesperson is confident and convincing. I agree with him.

Test yourself. Can you list at least five significant reasons to buy your product or to do business with you? Do you know what specifically is different or unique about your product(s) or company? Is there anything? Look to the areas of quality, specific performance characteristics, customer service, warranties, customer testimonials and pricing policy for possible answers. The more factual and detailed your answers, the more effective your sales and marketing messages will be. If you can't develop realistic reasons to buy from you or can't tell a prospective customer what is different about your company and your product or your service, you may fail.

Effective selling is like a good ad

Like a good advertisement, an effective selling process contains four major components: attention, interest, desire and action (AIDA). If you understand this process and the role of each step, selling is manageable by most everyone. It takes the personality and mystery out of it and stresses a logical process that moves the prospect from initial contact to buying the product. Any sales presentation or advertisement that ignores this four-step process will be less effective. Sometimes shortcuts sell, but why gamble, when a logical, well-thought out message aimed at the prospect's self-interest has a reasonable chance of success?

Attention

Attention is the beginning of the sales process. It's easy. You can get attention in a variety of ways, such as yelling, making a loud noise or placing a catchy headline or an outlandish photo as part of an advertisement. With all the messages that bombard people daily, you must use some effective means of grabbing attention.

Advertising experts understand the value of attention. They use eye catching colors on the packaging of products. They use television pitch men who yell at us. They may make outlandish claims about their product. They commonly use fear, sex, love and greed to appeal to our emotions.

Salespeople use a variety of techniques, from a simple offer of help to a high pressure phone call. Most people will listen for a moment or so, provided it is of interest to them. Getting attention is easy; holding it is the challenge. I think most of us get turned off by phone calls during the dinner hour with the solicitous "How are you this evening," as if the caller really cared. I frequently get calls from stockbrokers, some of whom are so persistent that hanging up is the only way to get off the phone. The person had my attention when I answered the call but quickly lost it because of his abrasive style and my lack of interest. Attention spans are fairly short and the professional salesperson knows that if you don't move the prospect quickly from attention to interest, there will be no sale.

Interest
At this stage of the process, the prospect wishes to know more, but has not made up his or her mind to buy. It is unlikely there will be a sale without interest. Most sales trainers agree that the most effective way of obtaining interest is by discovering the real needs and wants of the customer by asking specific questions. It is difficult to build interest without conversation. The prospect

must participate.

Most sales training programs stress the need to get the prospect involved in the presentation. Monologues by salespersons are boring and ineffective. Remember, if you want the prospect's interest, you must appeal to your prospect's interest, not yours. Questions do that. If you can uncover your prospect's wants and needs, you can tailor your sales message accordingly. If you cannot show how the product or service fulfills these needs or wants, you will not sell it to a prospective customer.

Seasoned salespersons know that to spark interest, the art of listening is more important than the art of talking. You must learn to ask the right questions, but be sure to carefully listen to the answers. A good salesperson is part therapist with a keen ear for uncovering motivation.

Desire

Up to this point, you have the prospect's attention and interest; now you need to create desire to buy your product or at least the desire to know more about it. To be successful, the desire must follow interest. It is at this stage of the process that interest may become a conviction that the prospect needs your product.

It may also be the stage that the prospect is fence straddling. The prospect is partially convinced, but unsure. A seasoned salesperson will sense this and reaffirm the benefits in the prospect's self-interest. This is a critical moment that requires skill in the art of persuasion. Budding desire can be as fragile as a flower. The wrong sales tactics can kill it. To intensify desire, you need a skillful reaffirmation of the advantages of buying and the reason for immediate action. A lost desire is a lost sale.

Action

The most important part of the sales process is action, for without it, there is no sale. All the effort and money you spend to gain attention and to develop some interest and desire mean nothing if the prospect does not buy. How do you get the action? By asking for it.

Most sales and marketing executives understand the importance of action and don't rely on the prospect creating it. Experienced salespersons will attempt to close the sale by asking for the order. Anybody in business who thinks the prospect will always ask to buy is mistaken. Sometimes in retail customers will ask to buy, but usually, if you are soliciting, the action is up to you. Creators of effective advertising campaigns or sales presentations build a message around a climax of action. Direct response television advertising asks you to call now and may even offer incentives to do so. Print ads that contain such statements as "Order Now," "Limited Offer," "Mail Today" or "Today Only" are examples of direct commands aimed at producing action.

You won't survive as an entrepreneur without selling your products. As noted salesman Red Motley said: "Nothing happens until someone sells something." Which are you most afraid of—failure or asking for the order?

Sales training: A mini-course

Learning to sell is fairly straightforward. Here is an outline of a step-by-step process long used by sales training executives that will help most anyone, including you and/or your sales staff, master the basics of sales.

Step 1: Prospecting

There are many ways of finding prospects (potential customers). You can advertise, you can do mailings, you can knock on doors or you can telemarket with phone campaigns. You can even buy lists of prospects. But whatever your method, prospecting means reaching out and contacting unknown possible customers. This step is difficult for many as you will encounter a lot of rudeness and rejection. It helps to think of prospecting as gold mining— being prepared to dig through many prospects to find a few golden customers. Expect a 90-percent rejection rate. Prospecting requires faith and fortitude. It is tough work! But it can't be avoided if you want to be successful.

Step 2: Qualifying

Don't waste your time on sales leads that have no use for your product or no money to spend. Just because you find people willing to listen to you does not mean they will make profitable customers. Early in my career I learned this lesson well after spending a full day in my car to keep an appointment with a Fortune 500 purchasing agent, only to find out his requirements were so small it did not pay to make the sales call. My disappointment and waste of time were my fault. When I called for the appointment, I neglected to qualify the prospect by asking the right questions. The prospect told me he used the product, but in my excitement to see him, I didn't ask the obvious, "How much?" A simple question and I would have saved a full day of travel.

With so little time in actual selling because so much of your selling day will be spent in travel and waiting rooms or in repeated attempts to contact prospects through phone, e-mail and other communication channels, you cannot afford to waste valuable time contacting the wrong people. As you will find out, time management is an important part of selling. To waste time is to waste selling opportunities.

Before you head out the door to call on that new sales lead, check it out. Be sure you are calling on the person who has authority to buy. Be sure there is a sufficient need for your product or service. And if selling on credit, be sure you will be paid. Remember to qualify is to question.

Step 3: Presentation
The heart of the sales process is your presentation. Think of your presentation as a persuasive conversation, not a lecture or monologue. Engage your prospect with questions about product use, problems, company policy on alternate suppliers and any other area that will demonstrate your interest in the prospect and your ability to serve his or her needs. To be effective and convincing, you must know as much about the products and services you offer as possible. Any apparent lack of knowledge will make it difficult to make a sale. If your prospect senses you don't know what you are talking about, you may as well close your attache case (or end your telephone call) and move on. People hesitate to buy from individuals or organizations they do not trust or have faith in.

There are many ways of delivering an effective presentation. The use of visual aids such as charts, graphs, photos and testimonials can help you stay focused and add credibility to your message. To tailor my presentation, I always involve any prospect by probing with a series of questions to allow me to uncover any special problems or areas of interest. An effective presentation caters to the self-interest of the prospect, not the seller.

To be successful at selling, do what the most successful do—listen carefully to your prospect. What he or she says is more important than anything you can utter. Listen and you will learn about the prospect's self-interest. If your prospect suspects you have little or no interest in his or her needs and/or well being, he or she will have little interest in dealing with you. You can't go wrong by catering or tailoring your sales message to the self-interest of your potential customer.

Step 4: The trial close

Assume your presentation (or phone call) is going well and you think there is some interest, but you are not sure if the prospect is ready to buy. You are afraid if you come on too strong you may get a negative reaction; so what do you do? A trial close. That is a question that tests the water or probes the degree of interest or even desire. A common method is a part-statement part-question, such as: "Assuming we get together, when would you like delivery?" The answer is noncommittal, but gives you an indication of how interested the prospect may be.

The purpose of the trial close is to discover in a nonthreatening manner, how effective you have been in creating interest. If the prospect is ready to buy, wonderful. If not, circle back to your presentation and try again.

Step 5: The close

This is the action part of the process. Without it, there is no sale. Yet, regardless of importance, this step frightens many salespeople because of the possibility of confrontation and rejection. Some salespeople actually hope the customer will close by asking to buy the product. It is the inability to close that is the downfall of many salespeople. They are afraid to ask for the order. It may surprise you to learn that professional purchasing agents who see sales people daily actually complain about those who will not get to the point and ask for the business.

How do you know when to close? Listen to your prospect. Pay attention to body language and facial expressions. Listen to your gut. If you try to close and get a resounding "no," try again.

Remember, selling is telling your story in a way that is so interesting to the listener that he or she wishes to hear more. To be effective, keep your message simple and in the interest of the listener.

Types of selling

Not all selling is the same. There are two distinct types of selling. The first is maintenance or repeat selling, which is selling on a ongoing basis to established customers, such as a retailer or distributor. The second is developmental selling, where nearly every sale is to a new customer, such as at an auto dealership. Sales and marketing professors or trainers rarely make the distinction between the two. Yet, the requirements and demands of each are quite different.

Maintenance

Maintenance selling is repeat sales to the same customer. It is an ongoing relationship between buyer and seller based on trust and reliability. High pressure sales tactics will not work. For example, if you own a small photo store and the sales representative from your major supplier is less than honest or pressures you to buy inventory you do not need nor can sell, you will soon be looking for another supplier.

If you plan on selling products to other businesses such as retailers or distributors, remember, their buying motives are based on the resale of your products at a profit, no other. As an entrepreneur, you will want to establish long-term relationships with your customers. You do this by honest and dependable dealings. Distorting facts, making false promises, not keeping your word and outright lies will lose you customers when they discover your questionable methods. As I have stressed, a long-term buyer-seller relationship is based on benefit and built on a foundation of honest and ethical dealings.

I once fired a salesperson for selling too much. Frank was very aggressive and continually pushed product on his customers who happened to be mostly small stores with limited resources. Because they trusted him, his inflated sales orders were rarely questioned. After a few months, most of Frank's customers were overstocked. Some were not able to pay their bills and others wanted to return most of the unsold merchandise. Because of Frank's overly aggressive sales efforts, business in his territory nearly stopped. Every store was loaded with our merchandise collecting dust. We had a lot of unhappy customers.

Frank was ill-suited for the job. He did not understand maintenance selling. Somehow, he thought selling was an arm-twisting, get-the-order-at-any-cost activity. He failed to grasp that when you routinely deal with the same customers, such as retailers and distributors, your success is dependent on their success—there is no sale until your customer sells the product. The real sale is the re-order.

Developmental
Whereas maintenance selling focuses on repeat business, devel-

opmental selling requires a strong closing ability as most every sale is based on finding a new customer. If you don't make the sale on the first call, you may not make it at all.

To be successful strong selling skills are necessary. You need to aggressively pursue sales leads, get in the door and get the order. Examples of these sales positions are auto salespersons, insurance agents, siding and window salespersons and real estate brokers. If you are starting a business where almost every sale is a new customer, it is critical you hire aggressive and money-motivated individuals.

Developmental selling is demanding. Unlike maintenance selling where rejection and verbal abuse are rare, developmental selling requires prospecting strangers who may be leery of you and treat you with rudeness, impolite behavior and rejection. It takes someone with determination, toughness and an enjoyment of the developmental selling challenge to be successful.

One of the secrets of this kind of selling is contacting enough people. The law of averages has not been repealed. If you make enough calls and ask for enough orders, you will do business. The more experience you get, the better you will be at it.

Persistence pays off

If you are new at selling, it is easy to become discouraged and question your sales ability. Rejection and less than polite behavior can be unsettling and even intimidating. A common mistake is to quit too soon.

When I was on the management staff of Capitol Records in Hollywood, the vice president of Special Products shared a personal story with me. His story began one day, early in his career, while calling on retail customers in downtown Los Angeles. He found himself with some spare time before his next appointment and decided to attempt to sell for the first time a large department store chain located a block away. When he met the buyer, he was told there was no need for his product as the store chain was satisfied with a competitor's merchandise.

Being in the same area the following month, he decided to try again. Once more the buyer told him he was not interested. With some free time three months later, he made another attempt. The buyer greeted him by asking abruptly: "Where have you been for the past three months?" Perplexed, he explained that on his two earlier visits he was clearly told there was no interest in his merchandise.

At this point, the buyer told him that he did not do business with any salesperson who did not make at least three but preferably four sales calls. He explained it was his business philosophy that he wanted to do business only with people wishing to do business with him and he viewed determination as a sign of future reliability. With that, he told him to get out his order pad if he wished to make a sale. He learned well that persistence does pay off.

Most purchasing agents know that buying from strangers, even brand-name products, carries risk. After the first order will they see the salesperson again? If there are problems, will they be handled in a prompt manner? It is only after a few visits and a demonstrated determination to sell will they be confident enough to place an order.

Unfortunately, when soliciting new customers in developmental selling, too many salespersons fail to appreciate the trust and determination factors and quit too soon. Various studies report that four out of five buyers will place an initial order only after the fourth sales call. Yet four out of five salespersons rarely get beyond the third call. They give up too soon. Thus, one in five succeeds by understanding the need to establish over a period of time a "persistent relationship" between buyer and seller.

Another major mistake is the lack of follow-up. How do you feel when someone promises to call you or send you something and they don't? When a salesperson follows up, a strong message of caring and customer interest is being sent. A salesperson who is diligent in keeping commitments and showing interest in their customer's well-being, will be a successful one.

Remember:
1. Fear of selling is based largely on myth and misunderstanding. If we go into business we must learn to sell as nothing happens until someone sells something.
2. Successful selling is not personality—it is a learned and perfected skill. You must not be afraid to ask for customers, business or money.
3. A sale requires attention, interest, desire and action. If you want the customer's attention, appeal to the customer's self-interest, not yours. Without desire there is no sale. Action means asking. Your biggest fear should be failure, not the fear of asking for business. Rejection is not failure, only "no" to your offer.
4. Ask questions to qualify. When presenting your product, listen to the prospect. To close, ask for the order. Don't quit too soon. It pays to keep trying.

Chapter 17
Hiring your sales people

Whatever you do, don't rush into hiring a sales staff. The story of Seymour illustrates just what can happen.

Seymour's sales force
Seymour's trip to Hong Kong was fruitful. He had managed to obtain the American marketing and distribution rights for the latest in a line of personal computer modems. Yet, he was nervous as he had committed to a substantial inventory. He was risking all of his financial resources, including his home equity. To sell such a large quantity of product, he knew he must quickly put together a large sales organization to sell to customers throughout the United States. Fortunately, he had experience in computer communications, as he had been the controller of an importer and distributor of similar products. He was aware of the size of the national market.

He knew it consisted of computer stores, mass merchandisers, mail order houses, department stores and electronic outlets. To sell to all these customers, Seymour faced a problem—how to assemble a national sales force? It had to be done quickly as any competitive advantage of the product could easily disappear due to the rapid changes in technology.

Although he was knowledgeable in collections, he did not have any sales experience. However, he was confident he could hire the right sales people. Seymour planned to function as the sales manager as well as the manager handling the finances. He did not need to concern himself with distribution and warehousing, as his cousin with a background in distribution had joined him.

As his former employer had used independent commission sales agents to cover specific geographic areas, so would he. Within a week, working under pressure at a breakneck pace, he signed sales agreements with enough sales agents to cover the majority of the market. Many of these agents were referred by former business associates. Some of the agents were just starting out and "hungry" for product to sell. Even though all his agents represented other companies as well as Seymour's, they assured him that his products would receive their full attention. He felt good. Everything seemed to be in place. As the first shipment of his inventory was expected shortly, he was eagerly looking forward to his first month of sales activity.

But it didn't happen. When the phone rang, it usually was a request for samples, lower prices or special credit arrangements. The few sales orders that Seymour did get were small. It was discouraging. Whenever he called asking about the lack of business, an agent's usual response was: "It takes time, I have a few things in the works, don't worry about it. Besides the market is slow right now." Frustrated and nervous, he became impatient and started yelling and berating the sales agents, accusing them of not being able to sell anything. When the situation failed to change, Seymour became despondent and threatened to "fire" the lot of them.

Shipments of inventory continued to arrive from Hong Kong, adding to his rising level of anxiety as all he owned was at stake. Not knowing what to do about the small trickle of sales orders, he sought the advice of business friends and was told to travel with his agents to find out what was wrong. The following Monday Seymour flew to Atlanta to call on customers with his Southeast representatives.

He returned Friday afternoon knowing he must make some changes. His commission sales agents were not working out. They did not appear that interested in his product; many had well-established merchandise lines that received most of their attention. He was even told by one agent that as Seymour's company was new and his product not a brand name, the agent could not afford the time and effort to pioneer an unknown item, regardless of quality or price. As he reflected on the frustrations of his trip, he realized that in his rush to line up sales people he did not take the time to find out what kind of sales organization he really needed.

Determine your needs first

Before you place the first sales help wanted ad, determine precisely what kind of sales activity your product and potential customers will require. Don't do as Seymour did and hire the first warm body that offers to sell for you. The selection and hiring of sales personnel is critical, as whomever you hire will affect your image and relationship with your customers. They are your representatives; what they do and say is a reflection of you. The wrong sales employees can cost you dearly in many ways. Don't assume that since you are only paying commissions, that the lack of sales is not costing you anything. Your poor judgment in hiring the wrong people is costing you lost sales opportunities and valuable time.

Study your customers. Learn how they buy. What do they expect in the way of sales service? How are your competitors selling their products? What is required in the sale of your product? Is it the kind of product that generates success through repeat sales? Or is it something that is purchased infrequently such as a new car, home airconditioning or capital machinery? How much technical knowledge is required to sell successfully? How aggressive must the salesperson be? How much experience do you require? These are just a sampling of the questions you must ask before writing your help-wanted ad.

The quality and competence of your sales employees or agents speak very loudly to your market about the kind of company you are trying to build. Your attitude and perceptions of sales people will influence your hiring practices. Will you consider your sales employees part of your company or outsiders only interested in themselves? Will you trust them to work independently or assume they spend the afternoons on the golf course? If you have managed a sales organization, you may wish to skip the remainder of the chapter. If, however, this is all new to you, pay attention. Developing and managing a sales force is very different from dealing with an office or production staff.

Match sales persons to sales jobs

Ask the person who delivers bread or nonfood items such as pet supplies to the local supermarket if he or she is in sales and you may be told "yes" as will the top performing advertising account executive. These are very different jobs with very different sales skills. The jobs are not interchangeable nor are the people. There is such a variety of sales positions that it is inaccurate to generalize. There are inside sales jobs, outside positions, jobs requiring strong closing skills, jobs stressing low-key reliability, jobs demanding persistence and follow-up and jobs based on technical expertise; the list is very long.

In Chapter 16 I noted that most selling jobs fall into two major categories: maintenance and development. If your customers are businesses, government agencies or other institutions that you supply a product or service to on a regular basis, then you need "maintenance" sales persons whose strengths are reliability, dependability, product knowledge, honesty and clear communication skills with modest powers of persuasion.

On the other hand, if you are continually prospecting and doing developmental selling in which each sale represents is a new customer, you will need individuals who are aggressive, who know the value of closing on the first sales call, who fight to prevent the prospect from leaving or hanging up on them and who are determined to get the order. If you are starting a business that falls into this category, such as home security systems, you need these strong sales types that are motivated by money.

Many sales positions such as consulting or advertising require a combination of the skills and talents associated with both types of selling. These require the aggressiveness necessary to obtain appointments and deliver presentations plus the reliability of follow-up until the contract is obtained.

Job description
Shortly after Eddie took over a faltering auto parts wholesaler, he ran an ad in his local paper looking for a salesperson. It was not specific, just "Sales help wanted, great opportunity for self-

starter." When Jason took the job, he was given a series of catalogs, price sheets, a lengthy list of gas stations and told to go make some sales calls. As Jason did not have any selling experience, Eddie was able to hire him at a very economical wage.

After two months, both were frustrated and ill at ease with each other. Jason was not selling much and did not understand what was expected of him. Eddie was impatient and convinced he had hired the wrong person. In the end, Jason lost interest in selling and Eddie was now sure all salespersons were lazy. This was a case of poor communications coupled with cloudy expectations. Eddie did not know whom to hire, nor did he know what the person should do.

Learn from Eddie. If you are going to hire an outside salesperson, be sure you know what they are to do. Prepare a job or position description. There is more to any sales job than just writing up orders. The position may require a knowledge of merchandising, customer sales training, inventory control and even some limited market research. You and your employees must have an understanding of what is expected. Don't leave it to chance. If you are unsure, go talk to some of your customers, explain you are about to add a new sales employee and get their opinion about the type of person they would like to see. Show them your preliminary job description and ask their comments.

I think you will be pleasantly surprised with the help you will get. Besides, it is great customer relations. But whatever approach you use, don't be casual about your hiring practices.

Select the right people
The wrong person can do a lot damage to your reputation.

Unlike your inside employees, salespersons are out in the market calling on customers without direct supervision. If significant distances are involved, your only contact for weeks may be phone, fax, e-mail or regular mail. How do you know what is "really" happening?

How do you select the right person? Besides intuition, do a background check with past sales managers, customers, credit references and any other source of information. Find out all you legally can about your perspective employee (since this is an area of change under the law, it's always a good idea to first talk to an attorney knowledgeable in this area of law). It can save you much grief. Don't make a decision based only on your initial impression of the candidate. You may be fooled.

Russell's ordeal

Russell, a friend of mine, found himself under investigation by the FBI because he had hired the wrong person. His nightmare started from a help-wanted ad. Russell was struggling to keep his company alive; he desperately needed sales and placed an ad in a local paper looking for sales and marketing help.

The first few people who answered the ad did not seem right. But then Vinnie appeared: dapper, well-spoken and very charming. He had all the right answers. He claimed many years of sales and promotion experience with a series of firms in multi-level and franchise selling, including being the director of franchising for a well-known entertainment company. However, because of a messy divorce, he had just moved to Florida and was now starting over. Russell was convinced Vinnie was the person to help him save his company.

Vinnie was a master at selling ideas. He thrived on it. The first thing he did was to promote the idea of multi-level selling by persuading prospects to invest in "distributorships." To attract investors, he placed classified ads in a host of weekly newspapers promoting exclusive distributorships that promised immediate high profits with little selling required. Vinnie assured each potential "distributor" that their investment in inventory was fully refundable if not satisfied in any way. Vinnie was smooth. His sales presentations were an art form.

According to Vinnie, all the new distributor needed to do was to place a prepackaged display rack with the inventory in various retail locations and wait for the money. He was a master at appealing to a person's greed.

For the first few months, everything was great. Money was rolling in from the "appointment" of distributors. Vinnie was collecting hefty commission checks and Russell was happy. It looked as it the company was finally going to succeed. But then disaster hit. The inventory was not selling at the retail locations. Distributors were becoming unhappy, some demanding to return the product and get their money back. To get the money to refund to the original distributors, new distributorships had to be found. Vinnie's plan had become a Ponzi scheme. Because of the initial success in selling distributorships, the problem "grew rapidly." The situation became desperate and Vinnie's promises more outlandish. It soon became impossible to refund everyone's money and the inevitable happened; complaints of fraud were lodged against the company. Vinnie took off.

Russell tried to honor the promises to the distributors as best he could to avoid any prosecution on fraud charges. He borrowed from friends, refunded what he could and quietly closed his business. He did not even have money to file bankruptcy. He still retains the experience as a bad memory and has no interest in being in any type of business.

His nightmare could have been avoided if he had checked on the background of Vinnie. A credit reference check would have revealed a long list of creditors chasing Vinnie. A few questions to the right people would have spared Russell his nightmare.

Hire experienced salespersons

With a new company you do not have the luxury of training individuals who have no selling experience; training is time-consuming. Your struggling company cannot afford nonproductive employees. Sales experience is not enough; whomever you hire must have a knowledge of your industry and product. If you do not have selling experience, certainly your first sales employee must; otherwise, it will be the blind leading the blind. Don't gamble with an unknown, untried sales organization. You need business now! Experienced salespeople with a customer following can save you much time and money. They may come with an established set of work habits that may not be to your liking, but the right sales person(s) bringing immediate business can mean your survival.

Don't fool yourself by thinking a sales candidate with years of experience and a customer following is beyond your budget; an inexperienced salesperson who will work for you "cheap" is false economy. It takes time and money to train someone. And it may be some time before you know if you have the right person.

Agents or employees?

Another consideration is whether you hire your own full-time employees or look for independent commission sales agents ("reps"). In many industries the majority of field salespeople are reps and if you are going to compete, you will wind up with such reps. Most have a following and can provide you with a quick entrance to the market if you have a salable product. But if you expect your reps to pioneer and develop a market for you, expect to be disappointed.

The majority of independent sales agents represent more than one manufacturer or distributor on a commission basis. They usually operate under contract as the exclusive agent in a given territory. As you might expect, they cater to their commission income. If your product is unknown, difficult to sell or appeals to a very limited market, don't be surprised if it is treated like a step-child. Your product will compete for the agent's time and attention with every other product he or she is representing. Most development activity for a new product is limited to an initial introduction throughout the sales territory to see if there is any interest. If minimal, the effort may stop there.

As agents represent more than one company and work for commissions, don't expect to control their daily activities. They are independent people and expect you to respect their independence. Your management role will be limited. They won't push your product to the point of jeopardizing their relationship with their customer following. If your product requires a hard sell to get it launched, agents may not be for you. Just because a sales representative wishes to sell your product does not mean much effort will go into it. Some agents hope that if they have a large product roster they may get lucky with a "hot" item.

Sales employees, however, unlike agents, function under your control. You can direct their sales efforts in the manner you feel to be the most effective. They are better suited for product introduction and market development than independent agents. You have more control over the content of your sales message and you do not have to compete against other products for attention. Their allegiance belongs to you.

The decision to select agents or employees will rest on the issues of control and cost. I favor experienced employees. Too many reps will take on any line of merchandise and fail to adequately attempt to aggressively sell the product. In doing so, the product line remains dormant. The rep has a contract preventing anyone else from selling the line; the company is essentially blocked out of the market. Valuable sales time is lost.

However, if you are going to use agents, be sure your agreement has a termination clause that allows you to cancel for failure to meet certain described objectives. You cannot allow fertile markets to lie dormant because of poor or incompetent representation. Furthermore, as you appoint your reps, make arrangements to travel with them calling on customers. It will give you an insight of how well your product may sell and potential sales problems. Be prepared to spend time training your agents. Don't assume they are well-versed about your products or services. You know what your sales message should contain; make sure they do.

A supervising tip for outside sales people

Unlike the inside employees under your daily observation and supervision, your outside sales personnel will function in an unsupervised environment most of the time. They may operate in a semi-autonomous manner, functioning to some extent in a manner they may feel most appropriate to the situation.

With such independence, the wrong person can do your business a great deal of harm. If they are unreliable, dishonest with you or your customers or spread false or inaccurate information, you will pay the price with customer ill-will and lost business. And it may be some time before you find out.

Tom's sales performance was average. He had worked for us just over six months selling stereo eight-track cartridges to our distributors in Tennessee and Kentucky. It was my practice as national sales manager to telephone customers at random. One day I was talking with our distributor in Louisville, asking how everything was going and if our salesman was taking care of his needs. He told me that he thought Tom was doing a great job as he phoned him every week for orders, although he had never met him. I became upset. I checked his inflated travel expenses and fired him. Tom was dishonest and had fooled us.

It is easy to be misled when you are not involved in daily direct supervision. As a small business owner, you would be wise to make random customer service calls to learn about sales performance in the field, as well as any other aspects of your business.

Develop a sales-minded attitude

What is your attitude toward sales people? How do you view their role in your company? If you have no sales experience and your background is, for example, engineering, accounting or production, you may have a prejudicial viewpoint. If you don't hold the selling function in high regard, it is time to become enlightened.

If you view your sales agents or employees as outsiders with little to contribute besides actual sales, you are distancing yourself from your market. They are the eyes and ears of your company. Since they are on the "firing line," they are the first to hear about problems, defects and advantages of your product, service and company. Many opinionated business owners ignore negative remarks by sales persons as excuses for not selling. Be sure before you assume such comments to be excuses. Don't have a closed mind to firsthand market information.

Do you have faith in the judgment of your sales employees? Some employers who have a "peddler" mentality think of sales people as dimwitted individuals who are hired to regurgitate a sales message without questioning its ethics, accuracy or validity. Such employers don't trust sales people or their judgment. Professional and socially responsible sales people don't stay long in such companies. They quit and move on to a more progressive firm.

How much control and latitude are you comfortable with? If you wish to encourage employee participation and creativity, then avoid a rigid sales management structure; such an environment is stifling and may discourage your better people from remaining with you. It also discourages any sense of opportunity. The message is clear: "You are an outsider and I don't trust you." On the other hand, too much latitude and too little contact sends the message: "I don't care"—not very inspiring to a sales staff.

To develop a dedicated and motivated sales force, treat them as professionals, be interested in them as individuals, be interested in their professional development and include them in your company plans. Unless you have had sales experience, you may not be aware how difficult and isolating the job can be.

Sales people can live in a negative environment. They hear the customer complaints (valid or not), they hear how much better the competition is and how lousy their company is. Add to that the long hours of follow-up calls and travel plus waiting for appointments that can all lead to discouragement and frustration. Create a positive work atmosphere to offset such negative influences. Demonstrating concern and showing positive recognition will work wonders in motivating your sales employees.

Sales employees must be positive and professional. The people you hire and how you manage them are a direct reflection of the way you do business. Sleazy employees will give you a sleazy reputation. If you believe that business is "war" and you hire combative, excessively aggressive individuals, customers will not welcome you for long. If your business requires repeat sales, professional appearance and behavior are critical.

Remember:
1. The image of your sales people creates the image of your business. Your sales staff is you in the marketplace.
2. Not all sales jobs require the same type of talent and skill. Develop a detailed position description. Match the skills to the sales job requirements. Before hiring, check out the candidate first! You need experienced personnel when you start out.
3. Determine if you need agents or employees.
4. Find a balance between control and latitude.
5. Treat your sales staff as part of the company, not outsiders.

Chapter 18
Financial management and performance of your sales people

You need to take a dollars-and-cents approach with your sales people. Begin by looking at your compensation plan.

Compensation: Paying your sales force

The word "commission" suggests opportunity for some and frightens others. From the beginning of the Industrial Revolution in the eighteenth century when sales people were called "drummers" to the 1950s, commissions were the common method of payment. Since it was believed the fear of failure and the desire for money were enough to drive a salesperson to succeed, owners and managers relied on commissions to attract and stimulate "hungry" sales people.

There are still firms that view sales people as "drummers," such as real estate brokers, investment brokers, telemarketing firms and a variety of direct sales organizations. In these companies, if you sell you are paid and the more you sell, the more you are paid. It's a simple arrangement: your worth to the company and as a person is your earning power. In David Mamet's play *Glengarry Glen Ross*, there is a scene where the sales manager is berating the sales force. He tells them they are worthless human beings unless they can "close" their customer leads. He brags that his wrist watch is worth more than the cars they drive. Not a very pleasant image of the selling profession.

After World War II, with widespread consumer advertising and the development of brand names and self-service merchandising, selling changed. Not everyone wanted high-pressure hucksters. And as many sales people were now college graduates, selling was practiced with a certain amount of professionalism. To attract such qualified people, companies altered their view of selling and threw out the straight commission plans in favor of combination base salary and commission packages.

Have you thought how you are going to pay your sales force? You have some choices. You may choose straight commissions. You may do as most firms do today, pay a base salary plus a commission or you can pay a straight salary. Your choice should depend on the type of business you are in and what is most helpful to your company's goals.

The common straight commission plan is a stipulated percentage paid on every sales dollar. The average ranges from five to 10 percent, but it may vary by industry, type of business and product. If you choose it, find out the rate for your type of business before writing your help-wanted ad. The prime advantage of commissions is that you minimize your risk. You are obligated to pay commissions only on actual sales and in some cases, only after you have been paid by the customer. This can be beneficial when you are starting out and must watch every dollar.

Another advantage is that it focuses on incentive, attracting those who are after dollars, not security. Salespersons who want large incomes will look for companies that offer them that opportunity; nevertheless, if they cannot make money, they will not hang around. It also attracts people who wish to be semi-independent—who dislike daily direct supervision.

A disadvantage is your lack of managerial control. You cannot order reps to see certain customers or focus on particular products. You cannot insist on nonselling activities, such as lengthy sales reports or market research. In effect, you cannot manage their activities as you do your other employees. Another drawback is the possibility of "runaway commissions." If you are fortunate enough to have a surprisingly successful product or service, you may wind up paying hefty commissions—even more than your paycheck. The following story illustrates an example of runaway commissions.

A Beatles mania commission story
Do you remember the Beatles before they were famous? I was a regional sales manager at Capitol Records in 1964 when we released the single *I Want to Hold Your Hand*, which was quickly followed by their first album. It was chaotic. Record dealers and distributors ordered in such vast quantities our factories could not press enough albums to keep up with the demand. Sales were so strong that most members of our sales force were topping their monthly sales quotas during the first few days of the month.

No one in Capitol Records had expected the Beatles to quickly dominate the American pop music scene. Their success was unparalleled; record sales broke all records. Our sales and promotion staff were in heaven; however, the commission portion of their income was spiraling out of control. A typical case was

Andy, a sales representative from New Jersey, who saw his average monthly income rise from $1,200 to over $6,000.

This was a classic case of runaway commissions. Management took action. If they hadn't, even the most junior sales people would be earning more than the company's senior executives. But why should they? After all, everyone in the record business knew the success of the Beatles was not due to the sales skills of the sales force, but an unexplainable set of circumstances creating a music phenomenon. As expected, management's actions were not popular with the sales and promotion staff. A few quit but most understood that the integrity and stability of the company was at risk.

Other monetary incentives
Quite different than commissions with its emphasis on selling, straight salary is used when the sales representative has little control over concluding an actual sale. For example, the representative may find a potential customer, make the initial contact, be assisted by engineers or other members of the firm and finally rely on a team for the final negotiations.

Straight salary is also used in low-level selling positions such as detail people who call on stores, take inventory and write orders for replacement merchandise. In such situations, the salesperson has no control over the actual sales of the product at the retail level. It is more a service function than selling.

On the positive side, straight salary limits selling expenses, permits control over the daily activity of the sales representatives and appeals to reps who want more job security. However, there is no incentive to sell. It attracts those more concerned with security than selling. If you need aggressive people with initiative, straight salary is not for your business.

A combination salary and commission plan is the most common one today. Structured correctly, it contains the advantages of both without the shortcomings. The salary is the base income, providing a degree of financial security and establishing the person as an employee, not an independent agent. It assumes managerial control over the representative's activities, recognizes seniority and includes nonselling, semimanagerial activities with periodic reviews and base salary raises. The commission income provides the incentive and rewards selling efforts.

Combination plans can be as simple or as complicated as you wish. Usually the base salary represents approximately 60 percent of the person's income with commissions representing the balance. With this plan, you can control income levels by varying the commission rate. Assume you are hiring someone to cover a particular territory that will generate $50,000 in sales per month. It is your opinion that the salesperson warrants earning $2,500 per month. You could establish a base salary of $1,500 per month, plus a commission rate of two percent. This type of compensation plan gives you control. You can avoid excessive commission earnings as your business grows by reducing the rate. Another advantage of combination plans is that you can equalize income levels amongst sales territories by establishing different commission rates.

Why should a salesperson lucky enough to be in a high volume territory due to the location of certain customers earn much more than some other salesperson who has a smaller territory?

Varying the rate creates an equitable arrangement for all. I have had arguments over this point. Some sales managers feel everyone should get the same commission percentage, regardless of territory. They feel that more sales volume is more work. I don't agree.

Besides the use of a base salary and commissions, some sales managers offer special bonus arrangements for specific accomplishments such as meeting certain targets or quotas. Or they may vary the commission rate, paying higher commissions on certain products to stimulate sales. Special sales contests, bonuses or trips are favorite incentive programs of managers and sales representatives.

But whatever you do, if you wish your compensation package to work, keep it as simple as possible. I have seen some programs so complicated that all they did was cause confusion and misunderstanding. A salesperson who feels cheated over a misunderstanding or confusing rules will not be in your fan club. When you design your plan, make sure it rewards effort—that it rewards those activities the sales force has control over, not luck or circumstance.

Sales management tracking tools
A sales force is costly. Depending on the size of your force, it can represent a major expenditure; you can spend between $50,000 and $75,000 per person. You hire sales employees to sell your product and earn you a profit. Are they doing both? It will pay to find out using a number of sales management tracking tools.

The direct cost of selling chart

There is an expense to selling a product. If the cost to get the sale is more than the gross profit, you will lose money on the order. If the cost of supporting a sales representative is more than the gross profit of that person's sales, you will lose money on your employee. You need to know if you have such problems. The direct cost of selling is a method to measure the profitability of your sales organization. The idea is simple. Add the base salary, the person's travel expenses plus the commissions and subtract the total from the gross profit of the salesperson's sales. This tool is helpful in analyzing sales performance.

Spend a moment with the example in Table 5. As you can see, if you are paying a base salary of $1,500 per month, travel expenses of $1,000, plus a commission rate of five percent on monthly sales of $10,000 (Column A), you lost money: the cost of supporting your salesperson was $500 more than your $2,500 gross profit or 30 percent of sales. On a sales volume of $15,000 (Column B), your representative made a minor contribution of $500. At $50,000 (Column D), the sales territory is profitable, as your sales costs have dropped to 10 percent.

Table 5
Analysis of the Direct Cost of Selling: Sales Person A

Item	A	B	C	D
Sales (mo.)	$10,000	$15,000	$20,000	$50,000
Gross Profit				
(25%)	$ 2,500	$ 3,750	$ 5,000	$12,500
Base Salary	$ 1,500	$ 1,500	$ 1,500	$ 1,500
Travel				
Expense	$ 1,000	$ 1,000	$ 1,000	$ 1,000
Commission				
5%	$ 500	$ 750	$ 1,000	$ 2,500
Direct Cost				
Selling	$ 3,000	$ 3,250	$ 3,500	$ 5,000
Profit or Loss	$ (500)	$ 500	$ 1,500	$ 7,500
Cost of				
Selling	30%	22%	17.5%	10%

The analysis is also useful in comparing the performance of your sales staff. Assume each column to be a sales territory. As you can see, you are losing money (or making little money) with salespersons A and B, whose sales are marginal; however, C and D are making a contribution to your company. Look closely at C and D. There are significant differences. C's cost of selling is 17.5 percent, netting you $1,500, whereas D's cost is only 10 percent, earning you $7,500. This type of information will help you stay out of trouble.

Another use of this method is to calculate minimum sales targets for your sales representatives. Or if you are thinking about hiring a new salesperson, you can determine how many sales dollars you need from your new hire to make it pay. If the market can't support that much, reconsider your plans. Make decisions on facts, not hopes. You don't stay in business by spending most of or all your gross profit on selling expenses.

If you find your gross profit is being eaten up with selling costs, you have three choices: You can: (1) replace the salesperson(s) with someone who can sell more, (2) pay the person(s) less or (3) find a way to increase sales without cutting prices. In any event, do something soon. If you ignore the problem or engage in denial, eventually you may have to close your doors.

Sales reports

Reports are a form of control. Not only do they keep you informed, they force discipline on your sales organization. To be effective, the reports must be informative and timely. As you might expect, most salespeople hate them! Too bad! If you don't require reports, start now. With portable computers and the Internet, it's easy for salespeople to send you daily reports.

The most widespread sales report is the daily call report. It is a listing of the sales representative's daily activities, which includes customers seen or called, products sold, reasons for not selling and a general commentary on the market. Since these reports are important, act accordingly. If you see interesting comments on the reports, respond. If a sales representative takes the time to write informative and constructive reports, he or she will expect you to read and acknowledge them. If you don't, they will assume you are not interested, which isn't very motivating.

Your sales force must understand the importance of the reports. It is not enough to demand the reports; the sales personnel must know why such reports are important. Your sales force is on the "firing" line and they know your customers' reaction to your product and service, good and bad. If you are to stay ahead of your competition, you must know the perception of your strengths and weaknesses. The more detail the better. Think of the reports as important as the *Wall Street Journal*. Study them, compare them; you will gain a realistic insight into your market-place.

Expense reports

Require expense reports if you pay your sales people for their travel expenses. If you employ your sales representatives on salary or combination salary and commission, it is customary to reimburse them for mileage, tolls, customer entertainment and hotels. Be sure to check the Internal Revenue Code for allow-able reimbursable expenses. But whatever and however you reimburse your employees, you must have receipts and reports.

Owners and sales managers frequently complain how difficult it is to get employee expense reports on time, which is surprising, as it is a report they turn in to get paid. Yet, sales people have to be nudged to turn them in. Many are months late, creating accounting problems. Insist on timely submission.

Follow these three suggested policies when it comes to sales travel expenses and you will save yourself money and grief:

1. No salesperson should absorb legitimate expenses and no salesperson should profit from his or her expense account.

2. No sales manager should use expense allowances as a way of supplementing any salesperson's income. The reimbursement of expenses is for legitimate travel expenses,

nothing else. Whatever your policy is toward expenses, it should apply equally to all. Avoid misunderstandings; make sure your policy is clear. Discourage any outlandish claims or luxury living at your expense. An expense account is not a bonus for anyone.

3. Insist on timely reports, accurate reports and honest reports. Let everyone know that a falsified report will get them fired.

How would you handle the following situation? I will never forget my departed friend Joe, known as "Broadway Joe" at Capitol Records, who during the late 1960s demonstrated a bit of creativity with a problem with his expense report. Joe was a colorful, warm and vibrant individual who created a razzle-dazzle Broadway image right out of "Damon Runyon." He loved plaid jackets and stylish hats. He was Mr. Dapper, with gold cuff links, wing-tipped shoes, colored shirts with white collars and cuffs and a stylish handlebar mustache.

Joe called on the large record stores and distributors in Times Square and mid-town Manhattan. He was the only sales representative in a 250-member sales force that covered his territory by taxi or on foot. One rainy windy day, as Joe hailed a cab in front of his office on West 44th Street, a gust of wind blew his hat off and down the street under the wheels of a taxi. On Friday, when he submitted his weekly expense report to Benny, his sales manager, you could hear the shouting throughout the offices. Benny told Joe in no way would he okay Joe's hat. The home office in Hollywood would never approve it. The following Friday the hat appeared again on the report, and so did the shouting match. This went on for two more Fridays. Every employee in the New York offices followed the battle between Joe and Benny with keen interest. Finally on the fifth Friday, Joe submitted his report and all was quiet. At first, everyone assumed Benny won. However, not one to give up, Joe attached a note to his report stating: "Dear Benny, my hat is in this report, you find it."

The call planning report

A sales representative who is professional and successful will plan his or her sales strategy and not leave it to chance. A call planning report describes that strategy. It is a report that lists by day, on a weekly basis, the customers he or she plans to see and even the goals of each sales call. The report is helpful to all. In preparing it, the sales representative thinks and plans how best to spend his or her limited selling time to generate the most business. In reviewing the report, management is able to evaluate and supervise the sales plans.

If you are paying a base salary, you have a right to know what your sales force is doing as well as the right to direct them. Generals don't go into battle not knowing where their troops are going. You shouldn't either. Call reports will tell you how effective your sales people are in planning and using their time. Do they make enough calls each day? Are they allocating their time properly? Bigger customers demand more time; are they getting it? A common complaint from smaller customers is that they are neglected. Is that happening to your customers? How often are different customers seen? Did you know that sales people can have favorites and can purposefully avoid others? You cannot allow that to happen; it may foster ill will with some of your customers.

David was my regional representative covering Baltimore, Washington and Philadelphia. At the time Dave worked for us, we did not have much in the way of sales analysis, but we did know that Dave almost always made his sales quota. He was responsible for 38 assorted distributors and retailers that he supposedly called on at least once every two weeks. Right after we installed a computer system that allowed detailed sales analysis by sales territory, we discovered an upsetting detail: Dave did almost 90 percent of his sales with just two distributors. One was his brother-in-law and the other a long-time friend. Dave must have spent a lot of time playing golf; he definitely was not covering his territory. We fired him.

Just because you hire experienced sales personnel, don't assume they are effective at managing their time. The more time your salespeople spend in front of buyers and the less time traveling and waiting for appointments, the more business you will do. Up to a point, the more sales calls per day, the more productive your people will be. You cannot afford to carry a disorganized, marginally productive sales staff. They can put you out of business. Expect the same amount of discipline and organization as you demand from your other employees. Insist on detailed call reports. If you have doubts or questions about a person's performance, monitor the report and make a few phone calls. You do not need a Dave on your staff.

Quantitative analysis: Quotas
What happens when you establish a goal and believe in it? You work toward it. What happens when you achieve it? You feel good about yourself. It will fill you with a satisfying feeling of confidence and self worth. On the other hand if you do not have any goals, you may get lazy and not care. Realistic goals

can be effective motivators, especially when there is competition. Goals can be like competitive sporting events. You believe it is possible and go for it!

A sales quota is a goal. It is a target you expect your sales staff to meet. It must be a target they expect to meet as well. Each must understand the importance of their target and how it fits in as part of your total business plan. To survive you must have a set of attainable objectives. When you lay out your business plan, hopefully, you construct forecasts and establish specific sales and profit targets. To meet these objectives, you do it the way you build a brick wall, one brick at a time; you reach your income goals one sale at a time. The sales quotas you assign to your sales staff are the building blocks to achieve your business plan.

The development of a quota system in your business can be either simple, guessing what each sales territory should do, or complex, such as constructing a detailed projection by customer and even by type of product. Whichever method you use, follow these simple rules:

1. Don't make the quota time period longer than a month or it will create procrastination and lose its effectiveness.
2. To be effective, quotas must be achievable, otherwise, don't use them. Quotas that are impossible to obtain are ignored. Unrealistic quotas will make you look foolish.
3. To stimulate all your sales staff, report everyone's progress during the month (or whatever time period) in percentages for all to see. It is a strong motivator as no one wants to appear on the bottom of the list.
4. Don't penalize success by pushing the top performer's quota out of reach. They may retaliate by selling less.

5. Don't use a quota system as a weapon to threaten poor performance. It will not solve the problem.

Quantitative analysis: Order call ratio/average order size
How do you know who is your best sales representative? Here is an uncomplicated way of measuring the sales strength of your people. For example, which of the following is most effective?

• Jack, who averages eight sales calls and obtains orders from two of the sales calls

• Bob, who makes six calls in a day but gets three orders or

• Charlie, who makes more sales calls per day than anyone else, but gets the fewest number of orders.

The order call ratio makes it easy to compare the sales efficiency of each of your sales representatives. To use it with one person will not tell you anything. You need to compare each person's performance so you can establish norms or averages that become acceptable bench marks for each salesperson. In the case of Jack, who makes more calls but sells less than Bob, it may indicate that Jack does not spend enough time on each call or the presentation may be too weak or hurried to make a sale. The comparison does not find solutions but suggests possible problems. Then there is Charlie, who is probably very busy, but not very effective.

By the way, the information you need to calculate your order call ratios by salesperson is right on the daily sales or call reports that you now insist your sales people submit to you.

The average order size is another comparative measurement that is helpful in analyzing sales presentation strengths. When you compare the average size of the sales order by salesperson, assuming similar customers, you will find your weaker salespersons will be getting smaller orders than their more aggressive colleagues. Consistent small orders suggest a hesitancy to push for more business or a lack of closing skills.

Combining the order call ratio and the average order size will give you a barometer of each employee's selling skills. If you have a sales representative who is writing small orders and has a low order call ratio, you are paying someone who lacks the skills to sell your product or is not making much of an effort to do so. If you have someone who makes few sales calls, but has a high order call ratio and turns in large orders, you have a winner, working part time. Such analytical tools make it difficult for poor performing sales people to hide behind a wall of excuses. You will not stay in business long if your sales organization is at the movies or playing golf every afternoon.

Ranking of sales volume

Our 80/20 principle is back again. Do you recall my comments about the 80/20 principle affecting inventory policy? I offered you the example of bookstores and best sellers. If you sell to many customers, big and small, on a routine basis, you will find that a small portion of your customer base is responsible for a large portion of your business. Or stated another way, on the average, if you have 50 customers, 10 (20 percent) of them will be responsible for 80 percent of your sales volume. Conversely, the remaining 40 customers will only give you a meager 20 percent of your business.

As you know, dependency on few customers is dangerous. To plan around the 80/20 problem, a helpful tool is the ranking of customer by sales volume. If you do it by sales territory, it is a tool for laying out the travel and coverage of that territory. A common approach is to classify customers by size (annual volume). See Table 6. A customers are the largest, B the next largest and so forth. The size of your customers and how much business they give you is valuable information to help you plan your sales and market strategy.

Assume you are selling your product to approximately 300 retailers throughout New England with sales ranging from over $100,000 to a few stores to many smaller stores buying less than $5,000 from you. Ranking and classifying customers allows you to "read" your market to see how to best serve your customers.

Table 6
Customer Classification By Sales Volume

Annual Sales Volume	Classification
$100,000 +	A
$ 50,000 - 99,999	B
$ 25,000 - 49,999	C
$ 10,000 - 24,999	D
$ 5,000 - 9,999	E
$ 0 - 4,999	F

Customer classification can be the key basis to sales planning. As your sales representatives can make only so many calls per day, how do they spend their time? The data helps your staff focus and plan their sales calls. In the example provided in Table 6, clearly A customers are more important to you than those smaller F clients. The usual approach is to schedule a call frequency pattern such as: A customers warrant a weekly sales call, B customers every two weeks and at the bottom of the scale, your F customers once every two months.

You must, however, avoid the danger of overconcentrating on your major customers and neglecting your medium and even smaller accounts. You will find that your large customers will demand more of you and some small customers, such as the F category, may be too costly to keep. A common solution to excessive selling costs and not enough selling time is weeding out small customers who are too expensive to service. Requiring your customers to do a minimum annual sales volume or you will discontinue calling on them is an effective method to prevent the accumulation of smaller nonprofitable accounts.

Remember:

1. Commission means opportunity to some and fear to others.
2. Combination base salary and commissions are "in." Avoid straight salary and straight commission plans if you can.
3. Know your direct cost of selling.
4. Insist on sales and expense reports and respond to them.
5. Be equitable with your expense reimbursement plan.
6. Insist on call planning reports.
7. Use quotas, but they must be attainable and fair. Report on quota progress. Analyze performance; use order call ratios and average order size.
8. Don't forget the 80/20 principle when ranking customers by sales volume. "Read" your market and rank and classify your customer base. Sales planning is critical for efficiency.

Chapter 19
Training, managing and motivating your sales people

Now that you've hired your sales people and set up some financial systems to track performance, you're ready to help shape your sales people.

Preparation and efficiency

Ask an actor what makes a successful performance and you will hear "preparation, preparation, preparation." Ask what makes a successful salesperson and you will hear the same answer. How do you prepare for success? An actor studies the play, understands the character and memorizes the lines. In the same manner, a salesperson learns about the company, understands the benefits of the product and finds the best way to present it. Acting and selling are much the same. Think of a sales presentation as a performance to an audience of one.

We applaud an actor's performance if it is realistic and convincing. Shouldn't a successful sales presentation be the same? To be convincing an actor must believe in the character and play the part with realism. Selling is the same. Only when your salesperson believes in your company and your product or service will he or she be believable. You are the playwright. You created the product or service and the script to sell it. Preparing your sales people to play the sales role is like a rehearsal that requires hard work and repetition. Successful "improv" is short lived. You are wise to leave little to chance.

I was wrong about Bob. When I interviewed him for a spot on our sales force, he convinced me of his strong determination to start a sales career with our company. He seemed motivated and eager to prove himself. Yet following a short burst of activity, his sales were mediocre. After months of attempts to improve Bob's performance, I was forced to fire him. He was the most disorganized sales representative I have ever worked with. He was never prepared. No matter what I did, nothing seemed to help the situation. It was frustrating to me whenever I traveled with him. To begin with, I was embarrassed to ride in his car; it was a mess. The ash tray was full, notes and rubber bands covered the visors, papers and samples were piled on the back seat and most disgusting of all were the empty styrofoam coffee cups on the floor. His brief case and sales catalogs were worn, dog-eared and covered with coffee stains.

During many sales calls he was at a loss to find what he needed. His inventory of sales aids was a disaster. He was unaware of the latest catalog sheets, price sheets or promotional material. In the past, as much as I attempted to help him become organized, any success was short lived. We worked hard to create sales and promotional materials to help our customers sell our product, but most of his customers never saw the material as it usually remained stuffed in his car trunk.

Finally, with no choice, I flew to Chicago on a Monday morning to fire him. I felt bad as he still did not understand why we placed such importance on organization and preparation.

Sales tools

To prepare your staff for success, get your people excited about your business. Share your dreams and plans with them. Tell them why you started your company. Tell them why is it different from your competition. The more they know about you and your company, the more they will share it with your customers. We all love success stories. So will your market.

Noted sales trainer Red Motley is well known for his statement "Sell the sizzle, not the steak." In other words, sell the benefits, not the product. To create that sizzle, your sales representatives will need selling materials, such as samples, catalogs and price sheets. Sales presentations without visual props can be boring. Do not just rely on the skills of a salesperson to get your message to your customers; dramatize presentations with sales tools. And, make sure everyone is aware of all your sales materials, especially if you have recently issued new catalogs, price sheets, ad mats or any other items. If you want an efficient sales force, you have a responsibility to be sure they are informed.

If you wish to find out if your sales force is up to date, hold a "bag inspection." The next time you travel with any salesperson, ask to see their sales presentation material. You will quickly discover how organized and prepared they are. If you find that your representative is missing catalogs, sell sheets or the latest price sheets, find out why. Is it your office that omitted sending the material or is a careless salesperson at fault?

Field authority

Eventually, an unauthorized promise or offer will cause you a problem. It probably will be about a special price, special credit terms or a return privilege. Such promises can cost you customers. How much authority you give your employees or agents to "wheel and deal" is up to you but be cautious. If you allow latitude, make sure everyone understands their limits of authority. Otherwise, you will have some costly problems.

Remember the story of Russell and his "star employee" Vinnie, who promised his distributors instant profits with a money back guarantee. He overstepped his bounds and the FBI knocked on Russell's door. There are many sales people in their eagerness to sell who will promise anything, leaving the employer the responsibility to honor it. You may not know it, but when a sales representative makes an offer, the customer assumes it is on your behalf. When the customer accepts the offer in good faith, you are responsible unless you issue certain disclaimers. Be sure your printed materials are precise about your terms of sale, including prices, discounts, freight allowances and return policies, if any. If possible, have your lawyer review the material.

During the mid 1960s a small manufacturer engineered a unique stereo eight-track tape player that had great sales potential. To handle sales, Nathan, the company founder, hired a network of commission sales agents in major cities. Within two months orders for the product by major retailers exceeded all expectations. However, none were paying their bills.

When Nathan called to collect money he discovered the sales agents promised the buyers a return guarantee. He was told that in order to get the product displayed in major electronic retailers, the sales agents promised the buyers that if the players did not sell, they should return their inventory at the company's expense. He was informed that he was not being paid because consumers were not buying the players. In fact, he discovered, most stores wished to return everything for full credit. With no money coming in and a warehouse full of inventory, Nathan's business failed. Unauthorized promises disguised reality and put Nathan out of business. Be certain that whoever sells for you understands the limit of his or her authority. You do not want any surprises that will bankrupt you.

Field travel

Field travel is an absolute must learning experience. If you spend a day visiting prospects or customers with one of your representatives, you will learn more about selling your product or service than a month of phone calls and meetings. There is no better way to obtain firsthand information about your market than by being there. If you are having successes, you can find out why. If you are having problems, here is a way to discover what they are before they put you out of business.

If you are thinking, "I do not have time to travel; I have too much to do for me to get out of the office," change your way of thinking. Isolation from the market place is suicidal. There is no substitute for accurate, firsthand market information. Rumors and opinions, if acted on unwisely, can bring costly decisions.

Successes

To gain the most, start by traveling with your most successful sales person. It will be an opportunity for you to see firsthand how your product is sold and merchandised. Successful sales and marketing experiences will better equip you to formulate future sales strategies. Remember, it is to be a learning experience; don't do any selling. You are not in the field to display your selling skills. It may be tough to just listen, but you must.

As you spend the day or days calling on customers, refrain from interrupting. Listen to your sales representatives and to your customers' comments. Try to observe the details of each sales call. Notice how your representative is treated. Pay attention to the relationships between your salesperson and your customers.

Study the sales presentations. Note the reactions. Focus on what advantages and benefits are stressed. How are your products and company presented? What sales techniques are used to promote the product? How is resistance overcome? Is there anything in particular that accounts for the success of your representative? Is there any special selling style that could benefit your other sales people? After your last call, spend some time and review the activities of the day. Discuss what you feel have been the rewarding moments, as well as any troubling ones. Ask for opinions and suggestions on how you can do a better job. Your sales representative will appreciate your personal interest.

Failures
A quick way to improve sales is by diagnosing the problems sales representatives have in selling your products. A few days in the field should offer some insight. Before you start out, you will find it helpful to prepare a list of topics and questions.

First, observe your salesperson's behavior. Is it professional? Question the representative's degree of motivation and commitment. Is the salesperson enthusiastic about selling your product? Does he or she believe in it? What kind of attitude does the person have? Does the person have any long-term goals? Is representing your business a job or a career position? Is he or she ambitious or content to coast?

If you find the individual has a lack of motivation, a poor attitude or a whimsical approach to life, advertise for a replacement. If instead, you look the other way, hoping for the best, the situation may undermine the morale and attitude of your other sales people. Successful and well-established firms may tolerate nonproductive employees, but a lazy person in a new business is a parasite.

Next, is the salesperson well informed? Does he or she have sufficient product knowledge? Is your employee up to date on company sales, credit and warranty policies? Do you have a general sense that your representative has sufficient knowledge to perform adequately in the field?

As you spend time with your representative, study the person's work habits. Look for clues that may explain the poor performance. Is the person organized? How well does he or she know the assigned sales territory? If your employee must get directions to a customer, become suspicious. Does your employee have your most recent sales and merchandising materials? Is the material organized and used properly? How well does the person manage selling time? In what condition are the employee's sales records—are they up to date? If you find the person is not organized and demonstrates poor work habits, write your want-ad unless you believe in miracles.

Finally, if you have a problem sales employee, pay a surprise visit. It worked for me. Tom's sales performance was always erratic. If we had words, he would shape up and do well for a few weeks, then slip back to his old habits. I was perplexed. I liked Tom and did not want to let him go, but I knew his on-again, off-again performance could not be tolerated. Frustrated and determined to solve the problem, I flew to St. Louis on a Sunday, called Tom that evening and told him to pick me up at my hotel in the morning. As he did not know I was coming, I suggested he not change his plans for Monday. When he arrived at my hotel, he asked which customers I would like to see. "Tom," I said, "Let's just go to your first scheduled sales call." When he said he needed to use the phone, I had my answer. Tom did not have a sales plan. We spent a part of the day together and it was obvious he was not organized and would perform only under pressure. I collected his credit cards that day. I have been criticized for my surprise visit approach as deceptive, even unfair. It may be, but as I said, it works.

Motivating your troops

To get someone turned on about your products or services, get the person fired up about your company. If you want your new sales employee to become excited about working for you, make sure he or she feels welcome and important. You will discover a sense of belonging is an important first step to a lasting and productive relationship. Do not overlook it.

Psychologists tell us that motivation is an inner-directed drive, whereas stimulation is an external stimulus. Yet, sales trainers and managers use the terms interchangeably. I agree with the psychologists that people who are motivated over long periods to accomplish goals are usually inner driven or "self-motivated." If a person is not motivated, you cannot create the motivation, yet you can stimulate them to action by using things such as fear, money and recognition. Unlike true motivation, stimulation is short lived. It needs constant reinforcement.

The poor success rate of many exercise and diet programs is that these programs are based on stimulation. If someone truly wants to lose weight and is inner driven or motivated, machines and meetings will not make any difference. If you want a motivated sales organization, hire motivated people and make them feel a part of your company.

However, do not overlook the role of stimulation if you wish to keep everyone at peak performance. As I have written throughout this book, for your business to survive you need to cut losses as soon as possible. If you have been fortunate enough to have hired the right employees, stimulating them should be easy.

Sales contests add a dimension of friendly competition that can be stimulating to all. They appeal to your employees' competitive nature, urging them to put forth extra effort to be recognized a winner. The reward must be meaningful and attainable, but it does not need to be costly; even dinner for two can be effective. It is not just the prize; it is the sense of winning and the recognition that goes with it. To make a sales contest work for you, follow these suggestions. It must be fair with everyone having an equal chance of winning. Keep the contest periods relatively short. People lose interest if they run over extended periods such as six months or a year. Frequently report everyone's progress. Award the reward as soon after announcing the winner as possible. Make sure everyone is aware of the winner. Play up the recognition aspect.

Bonuses can be stimulating. You can use them as a way of directing your sales employees to accomplish specific tasks such as signing up new customers, selling certain products or depleting surplus inventory. A bonus can create excitement. It is extra pay for extra effort. It not only rewards effort, but focuses attention on a particular activity. The nice thing about the use of a bonus program is that everyone can win.

Most of us loved to be fussed over. We like to be recognized and appreciated. Special awards, plaques, club memberships and special privileges are ways of acknowledging accomplishment and saying thank you. For example, are you familiar with employee-of-the-month award programs? They work. When you find a way of telling an employee thanks for a job well done, it boosts the morale of all. Everyone wants to feel important. I think you will find that if you reward and recognize your employees' accomplishments, they will respond with loyalty and dedication. Such efforts will help grow your business.

Leadership

Some sales people are strange. They may only respect fellow sales people. They may not like management, production managers, credit managers or anyone who says no to them, including some of their customers. They make their living by bringing other people around to their way of thinking. When they cannot do that, they may become negative and blame your company policies or product for their failures. The more aggressive they are, the more difficult they may be to manage. Leading such sales people may be a special challenge to you especially if your background does not include sales.

As you create your company, immediately establish your style of leadership. You may want your people to take initiative, but not control of your business. Find a balance between allowing latitude and suppression. If you have little selling experience, do not let anyone attempt to overstep their authority or intimidate you by claiming you do not understand the market. If you do not know how to deal with a situation, go visit some customers; you will have the answer.

Eventually you will experience a salesperson who can only sell if you give them special deals—do not fall for it. That person is not a successful sales representative. He or she survives by substituting special deals for selling skills. You must say no to these routine requests; if you do not, you will soon be "giving the store away."

When you travel with your sales people, do not take away your representative's authority by making a special deal during the sales call to prove you can get the order. If you do, you will embarrass your employee and force the customer to deal directly with you. Do not undermine your company policies to prove a point or impress an employee. It does not work.

Some sales people will think your customers belong to them. They get unrealistically possessive and believe that without their efforts your customers will go elsewhere. Do not believe it. If a salesperson threatens to quit and take your customers, do not believe that either. It has been my experience and it will be yours as well, that most customers deal with companies, not individuals. If you do have a productive sales representative that leaves you or whom you must terminate for some reason, do not worry. You may lose a customer or two, but you will not go out of business. To protect your business in such a situation, immediately phone each customer, thank them for their business, explain the change in personnel and assure them they will not be neglected. Your call will be welcome and you will keep your customer.

As you lead your sales organization, remember they are an extension of you, your company and your business philosophy. They are your living advertisements. Select and hire the best you can find. You will have fewer sales problems if you search for motivated individuals who are organized and share your approach to business.

Remember:
1. There is no substitution for preparation.
2. To be believable your sales people must be knowledgeable.
3. Personal work habits and organization are predictors of success or failure.
4. The use of sales materials is necessary to create the "sizzle."
5. Try a bag inspection to be sure your sales representatives are up to date.
6. Be sure your sales personnel know the limits of their authority. Unauthorized promises can be costly.
7. It is an absolute must that you periodically travel with your sales representatives. You must know what is going on in your market.
8. Do not tolerate troublesome or nonproductive sales employees hoping they will change. They won't.
9. To motivate your troops, they must first believe in you, your company and your product. Start by making them feel important and at home.
10. Stimulate to keep everyone at his or her peak performance. Use contests, bonuses and recognition.
11. Set the tone of your management style at once. You can not afford prima donnas on your sales staff.
12. Hold the line on your sales policies. Too many exceptions will weaken your marketing efforts.

PART FIVE
Strategies
for success

What is a strategy? It is an approach to a goal—your goal of a successful business venture that will reward you with your definition of success. You need to follow a set of strategies that will allow you to sidestep the potential "traps" that can bring your new business to a tragic ending. But staying out of "traps" is not enough; you need a strategy of success which is not just a business plan but a set of guidelines or principles that will help keep you on your path to success. Here are four essential ones that I have used and recommend.

- Strategy 1: Focus on a slow and steady growth. Control your growth: grow your business, don't explode it. Put your emphasis on earning a profit, building your assets, controlling your debt and managing your cash flow.
- Strategy 2: Diversify your customers for stability. There is safety in numbers; avoid dependency on a few big customers. Build a solid base of customers and products—be independent.
- Strategy 3: Decide whether to have partners, shareholders or investors; it may determine how and if you control the destiny and success of your business.

- Strategy 4: Don't give up. Think positive, think long term and hang in there. Only quit when you are forced to. Believe you will succeed. Don't think failure.

Chapter 20
Bigger is not always better

Big is better and more is never enough or so we think. We equate bigness with success. We'll hear people saying things such as "she is a big star," "he has a big job" and "they live in a big house." Whatever the reasons are for our fascination with it, do not mistake your new business's initial slow growth or its initial stability with failure. That is a mistake.

In the long run you need to grow your business, but establishing growth as your major goal can lead you into bankruptcy. Business bankruptcy court files have many stories of rapidly expanding companies. All too often when talk and plans of expansion begin to dominate the scene, seeds of destruction develop. Dreams of bigness can easily repress caution.

Before you attempt to peer over the horizon to see your worldwide empire, look at your inner motives. Is there a relationship of "bigness" to your emotional needs? What are you attempting to prove with your new business? If you are truly honest with yourself, you may not like the answers. Remember, self-examination is a lot cheaper than bankruptcy.

Small can be successful
Size and success are not synonymous. The size of the organization may have no bearing on its efficiency and profitability.

There are many small companies more profitable than their larger competitors.

In the United States, there are millions of small, well-run companies that earn owners a comfortable living. These are successful firms that have found a place in the market or their community. The owners or founders have learned to enjoy the fruits of their work or investments without feelings of envy because they are not a "Time-Warner." Not all entrepreneurs find the exploits of the "rich and famous" attractive. There are entrepreneurs who appreciate the value of a small business that is efficient and profitable with cash in the bank and few problems.

If your new business has reached a stable and profitable stage of development, think carefully before expanding. Will a bigger business bring you more happiness? If possible, try not to use the yardstick of "bigger is better" to measure your success. If after the first year or two you are still in business, you are a success. Perhaps there is a lesson for you in the following tale.

David's discontent

David was an unhappy young person driven by the need to prove his ability to compete and succeed in the business world. His father was a small business owner who operated newsstands in two New York City office buildings. In contrast, some of David's college friends came from wealthy parents who owned large and successful companies. As David told me the story, in retrospect he acknowledged feeling inadequate and ashamed of his parents. He did not want to be a small business person.

A few years out of college where he had studied business administration, he and a friend pooled their savings and borrowings to open a small printing company. The first year all went well; they earned a small profit and were able to take home modest salaries. Soon David's feelings of inadequacy surfaced. He was no longer proud of his accomplishments; he nagged his partner to expand regardless of risk and to look for larger customers. Anytime they had cash problems, David demanded they borrow. After all, he would clamor, "Big companies are not afraid of debt, why should we be?" He continually pushed to grow faster and faster. Whenever his partner became nervous, David laughed it off as thinking small. It was not, in David's opinion, worth being in business if the business was to remain small. As their debt and expenses grew faster than their cash flow from the increase in sales, they lost the business. Too many employees, too much equipment and too much debt caused it to collapse. They did not part friends.

Without profits: No future!

Without a profit the survival of your company is doubtful. The only way it can survive without earning a profit is by borrowing money or attracting new capital to pay the bills. As I wrote in the chapters on money, losses consume cash. Regardless of your short- or long-term plans or goals, you must put profit first. It is expected that during your first year and perhaps even longer, your business will secrete red ink. If you have planned for it, you will weather the storm. Otherwise, only loans or new investment money will prevent you from failing.

Here's a survival suggestion: after you construct your income or sales projections for the first year and you are certain it is a conservative estimate, reduce it by 20 percent. Why? Because the unexpected happens! For the same reason, review your budget or projected expenses, add 10 percent of the total and create an "emergency account." Contrary to the opinion of some, if you are cautious and underestimate your profit potential, you are not being negative, just careful. (See also Chapter 4 for more information on emergency accounts).

Do not apologize if you are making money. Earning a profit is not being greedy as some ill-informed, antibusiness people think. It is a margin of safety between your income and your expenses. In the long run, only profits will permit your business to flourish. Continual losses, no matter how small, will eventually close your doors.

Stay competitive: Stay alive!

One of the biggest "killers" of small businesses is complacency. Resting on your "laurels" and believing you have made it is a step toward failure. Complacency is like an insidious disease that slowly permeates the organization. Owners and employees become less motivated. Attitudes toward customers change for the worse. There is little innovation. There is resistance to change.

A leading accounting and consulting firm ran a striking television ad showing a weathered and deteriorating large sign on the roof of a factory with the words: "We Are Number One." Some of the letters were missing. The message was clear; management stopped caring.

Another possible example, was Kodak's loss of market share of the film market to Fuji. Kodak so dominated the market, controlling distribution throughout the film industry that it may have become complacent. Any place that sold film or cameras sold Kodak film. Agfa, a well-established German company, abandoned the United States film market after trying unsuccessfully to displace Kodak. Kodak's management may have assumed they could ignore Fuji's sales efforts as well. It appears to have been a mistake.

Future profits depend on your business being competitive. Profitable firms welcome competition. Incompetent firms hate competition. Monopolies, private or public, are criticized for their attitudes and inefficiencies. Over two hundred years ago the economist Adam Smith wrote his lengthy treatise on capitalism and the need for competition. According to Smith, without it we get lazy and assume our infallibility.

In many ways it is easier for a smaller firm to remain more competitive than large corporations. Decisions can be immediate. There is little, if any, of the red tape associated with multilevels of management. Turf wars are minimal. Policies and procedures are shorter and simpler. There is a flexibility inherent in well-run, smaller companies that major firms find difficult to compete with.

Small business owners are close to the actual market and able to see opportunities that cloistered executives miss. These opportunities may lead to discovering the "market niche" that results in your finding a comfortable marketplace for your business. Hopefully, you will learn that by staying competitive as a big frog in a small pond you may live very well.

The perils of expansion
Watch out if you hunger to quickly outdo your competition. A business is not a sporting event. Don't be fooled by the expression "The race is to the swift." Instead remember the fable of

the tortoise and the hare. It is not enough to start the race, you must finish it.

Peril One: I need more sales—now!

An increase in your sales volume may be a misleading measure of growth. What caused it? Did it increase from market conditions, expensive promotions, reduced prices or very loose terms of sale? What will it do to your profits?

If you have been fortunate to find a certain market niche that propels your business ahead with a healthy and steady growth, hooray! But if you are forcing it by giving away your profits, what are you doing?

For example, when you offer a promotional discount off your selling price to stimulate sales, are you aware of the impact it will have on your profit? Did you know that a mere 10 percent discount may require you to sell as much as 50 percent more to earn the same profit?

Hypothetically, assume your new company is selling $50,000 a month of merchandise earning you a 25 percent gross profit of $12,500. If you reduce your selling price 10 percent, with no increase in sales, your gross profit will fall $5,000. To recover it, you must boost sales by $20,000, which is almost 50 percent to earn the same amount of profit.

Any increase in promotional expenses may be costly to your bottom-line. According to a highly-respected former executive of Capitol Records, "Buying business is expensive."

When the Japanese industry invaded our consumer electronics

industry, their goal was to capture as large a market share as possible and as fast as possible. American firms were driven from the industry because it was no longer profitable to remain. Sony and Panasonic became household names. How did they do it?

They had financial subsidies from their parent banks. The strategy was simple; in fact, it was adapted from the strategy that built Standard Oil before World War I. These companies loosely copied American products and entered a particular market with low prices (keeping prices high in other markets) and absorbed the losses until they forced competitors to leave the market. Once they acquired a significant market share, they slowly pushed up prices. Ironically we applauded their efforts and complemented them on their "long-term outlook," while faulting American management as being short sighted and too concerned with quarterly profits and Wall Street.

If you wish to follow the Japanese model, do so, but arrange for a financial backer with deep pockets and much patience before you start. This is not a good model for most small business owners.

Peril Two: I need more people

My friend Murray was fond of saying: "Any fool can hire more people." When I started my first business I quickly found out what he meant. I found it was easy to confuse hiring people with growth. Adding employees in anticipation of expansion and customer demands is wise in certain circumstances but not usually with a struggling new enterprise. It may be foolhardy to hire on a perceived need arising from hopeful growth. Watch out for wishful thinking. Add to your staff when you have an increase in necessary and productive work loads, not busy work!

Any increase in expenses has a more than proportional effect on your bottom line. If you have a 10 percent net profit, then for every additional dollar you spend on new employees you must sell an additional $10. A new $30,000-a-year employee means $300,000 in new business is necessary to retain your profitability.

Let real growth stretch your staff! Increase your business first—then your employees. Welcome complaints about "too" much to do. It may signify your people are working at near their maximum efficiency. This may also be a good time to evaluate and prioritize employee work activities, eliminating low-value tasks whenever possible.

Peril Three: More locations

If you are intent on expanding into new market areas, you may have the urge to establish new locations regardless of immediate prospects. The result of a premature, ill-planned expansion can be a growth in expenses that may drain your cash.

Anytime you plan to expand your business where it requires you to add to your overhead or fixed expenses, be ultracautious. Put your plans on paper. Estimate how long it will take the new location to generate a positive cash flow. You can lay off people and you can return or liquidate surplus inventory, but unprofitable new facilities with leases or mortgages are problems not so easily resolved.

Peril Four: Following your competition

Be cautious about following the actions of your competition. Do not allow the destructive emotion of envy to impair your business judgment. Do not worry about missing out or being left behind. The outward appearances of any situation, competitor or friend can be misleading. For all you know, your competition may be overextending itself and planting the seed of its destruction to your eventual benefit. Do some market research to find out if your competition is really that successful. There is much to learn from a stable and successful competitor but much danger in following one headed for possible bankruptcy.

If your customers brag about your competitor's pricing and terms, become suspicious, as it may be their negotiating strategy to get a better deal from you. It is a common technique. If your customers are applauding the merits of your competitor's product, be sure the comparison is comparable and not simply comparing "apples with oranges."

Before jumping to copy a competitor's plans or product and discarding your own, test and research the situation as you may be more correct than you realize. Self-criticism is easy.

Three growth strategies
Here are some effective ways to help your business grow.

Let your success grow gradually
It can be difficult to judge the right amount of growth you will need to insure your long-term success. If you try to grow too fast it can lead to your insolvency. If you repress growth, it can mean you are missing opportunities. Here are a few hints to help you set the right pace:
1. How fast is your industry growing? Are you keeping up with it?
2. Be cautious of your short-term liabilities outpacing your short-term assets.

3. Increases in your expenses should lag behind any growth in sales.
4. Be cautious of mortgaging your future. Your survival during the first three years means you must be as financially flexible as possible.
5. Don't always view retrenchment as failure; it may mean survival.
6. Be comfortable with your rate of growth. Your business is not a sports event.

Think and act long term and react accordingly
Being in business is as much an emotional experience as it is financial. Just as it is easy to be exceedingly optimistic, it is as easy at times to be discouraged and think your business is headed for ruin. I do not know any entrepreneur who has been lucky enough not to suffer problems and setbacks. Unless you are the exception, you will as well. Try not to listen to the demons in your head at these moments. If you handle your problems correctly and as rationally as possible, they will pass.

Have faith. Believe you are going to be in business a very long time. Avoid any belief that you will fail. Do not view your business as temporary. Avoid a "wait and see attitude." As I wrote in Chapter 12, it is important you make an emotional commitment to the success of your business. You will feel more confident. You will make better decisions.

Nevertheless, even with a long-term outlook of permanence, you must keep a sense of urgency. Do not confuse my statements with a false sense of security. You need to maintain and feel that "sense of urgency" to quickly move your new business from losses to profits.

Develop an inner-directed business

Starting a business is a creative activity. You are giving birth to a new entity. You are creating an organization that contains you. As it develops, it will reflect your personality and value system. Just as you have an inner-voice you may call intuition that helps you with your choices, your new business has an inner-voice that will reflect the attitudes and personalities of all your employees. If your employees are positive and committed to the success of the venture, you have a better chance of realizing that success.

Along with a business having physical and financial assets, it also has intangible characteristics. Some refer to these as the personality or the spirit of the organization. It's also called the "corporate culture." Some companies are happy places; others are not. People, not the product, create the environment.

As the owner of the company, the attitude and outlook of your employees must begin with you. You must be an inspiring leader. You must enjoy your creation. You must enjoy being in business. If you do not and wish you were somewhere else, so will your employees.

Remember:
1. Plan and pace your growth: don't wish it, don't rush it and don't repress it.
2. Instant gratification does not belong in business.
3. Your business is not a sporting event. You do not have to be first.
4. Without profits, market leaders become market losers.
5. Remember, complacency kills businesses. Don't lose your "sense of urgency."

6. Buying business can buy you bankruptcy.
7. Plan to leave your business to your grandchildren—i.e., plan to be in business for the long haul.
8. Create a positive "can do" spirit in your business and remember, it must start with you.

Chapter 21
Diversify customers, markets and products

Diversification has advantages. In our society our cultural diversity brings many diverse lifestyles and cultures together for a rich and interesting population without one dominating all others.

In matters of money, financial advisers will tell you to diversify your savings and retirement dollars into a variety of investments to minimize your risk. For similar reasons, corporations may diversify by buying companies in nonrelated industries.

The goal of diversification for your business has the same objective: to reduce risk by avoiding dependency. To remain in business, you must strive to insure that no one customer and no one supplier is in a position of "controlling" your company. You will lose control if you allow your business to be "held hostage" by a powerful customer or supplier. You will have turned your business into an "employee." It can easily happen. There are countless stories of small companies falling victim to the temptation of the comfort and ease of catering to the big customer.

Diversification: A strategy of survival
The advice "do not put all your eggs in one basket" warns us of

the danger of dependency. Remember the earlier story of Frank and his one customer—it nearly put him out of business. He thought things would never change. The ancient Greek philosopher Heraclitus left us with the enduring message: "The only permanent thing in life is change." We change, our customers change, our markets change and our products become obsolete from change. Nothing is stagnant—except perhaps dying firms and institutions. The anticipation of change should be part of your business planning. At the moment, you may have the most wonderful customer, but what if your customer fails? What if your customer is bought by another company? What if the purchasing agent quits? So many things are possible that dependency on a single customer or product is foolhardy and dangerous to your survival.

I witnessed just such a dependency that nearly destroyed a company. During the late 1960s I owned a sales and marketing agency representing a group of record companies including Sun Records of Nashville. The Sun label had recently been bought by Shelby Singleton from Elvis Presley's manager, Col. Parker. The ownership of Sun gave Shelby the recording and publishing rights to some of the early rock and roll favorites recorded by such artists as Jerry Lee Lewis and Johnny Cash.

At first, all went well. After rearranging the material and designing new cover art work, these old favorites went on to a second market life. Nevertheless, after two years of aggressive selling efforts by the sales manager, the demand dried up and the market became saturated. Now Shelby needed new talent.

At the right moment, country singer Jeannie C. Riley walked into Shelby's life with "Harper Valley PTA." When Shelby finished the recording session, he supposedly commented to his recording engineer, "This is a good country record." He did not realize at the time he had produced what would become one of the biggest record hits of his career.

Sun Records exploded. "Harper Valley PTA" was played on radio stations everywhere. It was an instant top 40 hit. The money flowed in. Record distributors flooded Shelby with orders. He expanded his company overnight into a miniconglomerate. He built a studio, bought a record pressing plant and dabbled in creating a theme park, as well as buying my company. He told me at the time that he had waited all his life for such an opportunity.

He was confident his luck would continue. He gambled on Jeannie C. Riley recording another top-selling album. However, it did not happen. There was little air-play of the new album, leaving no hope of creating a much needed "hot" single from the album. The new album was dead. Jeannie C. Riley's moment of stardom appeared over. The party at Sun Records was over. It had been a one-artist-one-hit-single party.

If I remember correctly, to prevent bankruptcy, Shelby sold his record pressing plant, found a way to lease out his studios, abandoned his theme park project and shut down my former company. Finally, it was only Shelby's charm that kept his creditors at bay. His company is still in business but in a much different way without the overdependency on one artist.

Set a goal of customer diversity

From the beginning, promise yourself that your business will never be dependent on any one customer. Establish a personal conviction that you will work to insure that as soon as possible, no one client will control more than 20 percent of your sales volume, even less if you can. I am not saying to refuse to do profitable business with your best customer. I am suggesting you find more customers without delay.

If you can exist with a few customers, you may find it easy to yield to the temptation of a comfortable existence without looking for new clients. Unless you like the challenge of selling and are sales minded, you may have to push yourself to aggressively seek new markets.

If you do not like to sell, you can find many excuses not to. For example, it may not be easy for you to switch mind-sets from such possible future problems as cash shortages or collections to "everything is wonderful, buy my product." Or if there are other tasks you prefer doing, it will be easy to procrastinate. And if business is "good," you may think: "Why bother, I have to take care of my present customers. I will look for new ones later."

As you will find out, if you are selling to the industrial or commercial market, it will take time to get your first order, twice as long as you think. Potential customers will want assurances your company will be around in the future and that you will honor your commitments. Be prepared for delay. Do not wait until you are in trouble; it may be too late to change the situation.

If you can say no, you can survive
If your most important customer knows that you are vulnerable without their business, in due time they may make demands you cannot meet if you are to stay in business. You may not be able to refuse without closing your business. In contrast, if a

small customer presents you with a similar demand, it is easy to say no. The auto and electronics industries are strewn with the bones of small subcontractors who relied on a few customers.

The new management philosophy of "single sourcing" outside manufacturing requirements is supposedly based on building a closer relationship with vendors. Instead of obtaining the same product from three or four suppliers, the new thinking is to find one and work closely with one source. I believe such customers want more control over the production and pricing policies of their suppliers. They are well aware of the importance of dominating the production capacity of small firms.

If you find yourself in this position, you will discover it difficult to turn away the business. It may be in your best interest at the present to take this business, but it can be unprofitable over time with the additional concessions you will have to make. When customers dominate you they can dictate to you. I advise you to use your temporarily prosperous present situation to plan and start your strategy to get out from under the umbrella of dependency as soon as possible.

Establish the goal of a broad-based market foundation
There are many ways to expand your customer base. To begin with, you can start soliciting new customers. If you cannot do the selling yourself and you can afford it, hire a salesperson. If you do so, be willing to spend the time and effort to prepare your employee to be successful. If training is too burdensome, you may wish to find a person with experience in your product or industry. That person may have a customer following from which you can benefit. While he or she may initially be more costly, that may change over time.

Another way is a minor form of diversification. Assume your business makes a nonproprietary product for a few large customers (such as manufacturing the metal chassis for a brand-name computer). Ask yourself: "If I can succeed in one market, can I use the same approach in a different one?" It will require finding new customers and perhaps even new equipment. However, the alternative is to remain as you are.

Looking for new ways of distributing your product may get you new customers. The following example illustrates how it is possible to take a different version of the same product and sell it in a different market.

When the prerecorded, eight-track tape cartridge was introduced in 1963, record distributors and music stores rejected it. Eight-track tape manufacturers paid small royalty advances and negotiated the right to manufacture and sell (in tape format only) the album catalogs of various record companies. Some record "mavens" dismissed the importance of these tape companies as they knew nothing about the music business. However, they surprised the music industry by creating their own channels of distribution in the auto and electronics markets.

Knowing they had mistaken the marketplace and frustrated by losing control of a new market to "outsiders," leading record labels such as Atlantic and A&M fought to recover the tape rights to their own catalogs.

Another example of selling to new markets is the merchandising of automotive parts in nonautomotive stores. This is but one example of finding success with new distribution outlets for "old" products. Mass merchandising and self-service packaging have created new avenues of marketing for many products. Let your imagination run with such possibilities for you.

Amway and Mary Kay were built on the premise of finding new markets. Instead of depending on stores to sell merchandise, they did an end-run, selling directly to the consumer.

In a similar manner, think about using television advertising. It has opened up opportunities for small unknown companies that could not sell to established distribution channels. The products of these companies have ranged from household mops to wrenches. Such firms were told by wholesalers and mass merchants that as their product was unknown and had no track record, they were not interested in it. I like the reverse psychology of the advertising message from such firms, boasting: "Not Available in Stores." It is an interesting twist on rejection.

Mail order advertising may hold promise for you as it has for others. There is a chance you can discover such possibilities by looking at the variety of merchandise for sale in the response ads of many magazines. You may pick up some profitable ideas. If you do, it is possible to do market tests with minimal risk. If you think you have a product that may appeal to a reader response market, try it. However, do not limit your efforts to a single ad. Test a number of publications and types of ads.

Plan to lose your best customer

If you think planning to lose your best customer is defeatist, think again. It is planning a defensive strategy against your vulnerability. As you know, nothing lasts forever; your best customer may leave tomorrow. Be prepared for it. Customer attrition is unavoidable.

To start with, do you know the percentage of your business that your largest customer represents? If you are busy worrying about your bills, your checking account balance, your inventory, your employees and your production, it is most likely a detail you have not had time to ponder. If you think such a detail is unimportant, you are mistaken. (See p. 217 in Chapter 18 to see an easy way to calculate customer volume.)

Next, play "what if." Review your last three months sales and subtract the amount of business from your largest or two largest customers. What do you have left? Ask yourself: "Is it possible to cut expenses enough to permit my business to exist without these customers?" If the answer is "no," you must plan to find a way out of your "possible" problem before it develops.

Using most any of the many computer spreadsheet programs available, such as Quattro or Excel, it is easy to create all types of "what if" scenarios. It is a painless way to explore best-case and worst-case situations. Seeing the results of your or your customers' actions on paper will help you avoid wishful thinking that can obscure your perspective. Furthermore, if you know how important each customer is to your business, the knowledge will help you with your decisions. I know I find it valuable.

Just such information swayed my business associate from making a tactical mistake with the future of the our first branch location. A few months after we opened in Tampa, Florida, our major customer requested a meeting with our chief executive, John. Sensing an opportunity and overestimating their importance to our Tampa facility, this customer issued us an ultimatum: either we allow them to become partners or we lose their business. John was upset. At first, it seemed that the loss of the customer would force us to close the branch. Fortunately for us, their psychological presence was larger than their dollar presence. After John did a sales volume analysis, it was apparent we would lose business but not enough to put our branch out of business. John called the customer and said, "No thanks."

A few months later, seeing that we were doing fine without them, they returned and have remained a customer. With knowledge, John replaced his fear and worry with confidence and definitive action. Ignorance can cripple your business; it will lead you to fear, worry and wrong decisions.

If possible, stay aware of your competition's problems with customers. You may discover your competition is in a similar situation of possible customer loss. This could be an opportunity for you. Why not solicit their unhappy customers? Just as customers need a reason to do business with their suppliers, they also need a reason to leave. Perhaps you can offer your competition's customers a reason.

Set a goal of product diversity

A single product may be as risky as a single customer. A product life cycle is similar to the problem of customer attrition. Products rise and fall in popularity. What was popular yesterday is obsolete inventory today.

No matter what product you sell, eventually it will be out of date in appearance, form or performance. Technology and fluid consumer tastes are speeding up the rate of change that affects all products in all markets.

Yesterday's best-selling novel is now at a close-out price.

Yesterday's top box office attraction is now available in your local video store. Yesterday's "state-of-the-art" computer is today's doorstop.

Just as certain products lose sales appeal, other products gain. The product life cycle can cause failure and can create opportunities. While no product is exempt from the life cycle, the length varies from a day (daily newspaper) to decades (passenger rail traffic). CB transceivers are in the final stage of decline whereas wireless phone communications are still in the growth stage. Look around and you will find numerous examples of products moving throughout their life cycle.

Perhaps you may find new uses for your product that will lead you to new markets. Many products have crossed over from industrial markets to consumer sales. Portable power hand tools, pressure washers, paint sprayers and home alarm systems are examples. There are few quick answers to finding new uses; but try, you may get lucky—many other companies have.

Let me offer you a note of caution. If you are going to create your own brand-name product as a way of finding new sales opportunities for your company, be sure your plan is well thought out. One slip can bankrupt you. It is not easy to develop and nurture a product that requires extensive promotion and marketing. Brand-name acceptance by mass merchants is very costly. It is not a realistic goal for a small company with shallow pockets. Be even more cautious if you have little experience in merchandising and marketing.

Even if you have the right idea and the right product, test market it before committing your company's resources. Even assuming you are the world's most brilliant engineer, you may lack the understanding and the amount of money necessary to sell your creation. Do not hesitate to reach out to more knowledgeable people for guidance. Beware, too, if your product can be easily "knocked off"—copied by other larger companies, even if you've trademarked or patented it. As I have suggested before, watch out for wishful thinking.

Plan your product's funeral
Just as I have urged you to look for new customers, you must look to the future of your company with new products or services (or new uses for them). Although you may have an extensive product line, plan for its demise. Start looking now.

Do the same type of analysis with your product sales that you would do with your customers. Play what if. Remove your best selling item from your sales—can you keep the doors open? Ask yourself how long will the present success of each product last?

Your analysis will be your best assurance against failure. It should tell you how vulnerable your business is and if you have any foresight, how much time you have with your present products or services. I caution you against rigidity and the refusal to accept change—it will doom you.

The answer may be within
Let me share two events in my business career that proved to me the value of looking within your own business for some surprising answers.

In November 1968, as a result of my experience with the marketing of Capitol Record's eight-track tape product, I was offered the position of vice president of Marketing at International Tape Cartridge Corporation. Through legal maneuvers and contract expirations the firm had lost the tape rights to much of its best-selling talent, including such recording stars of the era such as Aretha Franklin, Herb Alpert and The Supremes. With a much diminished catalog, the new president of the company was worried about the company's future.

Initially, I was reluctant to join the company, but after seeing the long list of record companies the firm had contracts with (in many instances, never releasing the material or making any effort to sell any of the product), I saw opportunity.

During my first six months on the job, I recruited a national sales organization that included a dozen Capitol Records salespersons with experience in the new tape industry. At the same time, I pressured the operations manager and the artist and repertoire director to release dozens of albums from the many dormant labels for which we had the rights.

Within a year with our "new" catalog and our seasoned sales force we became serious competition to the industry giant. When I left the firm a year later to form my own sales agency, the company was at its peak. The ingredient of its success was in the "unexciting" dormant catalog that earlier management had overlooked.

Ten years later, I started Adams Magnetic Products, thinking I could design and sell a line of blank audio cassettes in competition against the likes of TDK and Maxell. I was mistaken. Within a few months I was facing disaster. My product was fine, my prices competitive, but consumer perceptions were not; the product did not move off the shelf. Consumers rejected it. I tried everything—ads, displays, promotions, special packaging of the product to encourage impulse buying, but nothing helped. I even experimented with unique distribution channels such as tobacco wholesalers who distributed all types of consumer items to a wide variety of stores. I met with failure.

I well remember that Sunday afternoon in late January, 1982, when I was working on my financial records and realized the product being returned to me by my customers was more than my sales for the month. It was a moment of bitter truth.

Discouraged and depressed, I searched for any possible avenue to sell my product, even looking through the yellow pages hoping for an idea. Eventually I stumbled upon the industrial audio-visual market and found if I packaged the audio cassettes with the distributor's imprinted name, the distributors would distribute the product to schools and industrial users. Two years later, this approach led to similar private-label packaging for various United States government agencies, such as the Secret Service, Social Security Administration and Drug Enforcement Administration. Within a year following the first federal government sale, Adams Magnetic Products obtained a General Services Administration contract.

Around the time of my near disaster with my tape business, I came across a wonderful little inspirational book entitled *Acres of Diamonds* by Russell H. Conwell. Even though his examples are dated, his message is not.

He wrote of tragic outcomes in the lives of individuals who had turned their backs on their own resources to venture off to some unknown and distant destination because they could see no future with their present situation. He warned his readers of the folly of "the grass is always greener on the other side of the fence." In one such story he describes a wealthy Arab gentleman who, lusting for diamonds, sells all he owns to prospect in distant lands. And what happens? The buyer of his property discovers diamonds in abundance.

He wrote: "Had Ali Hafed remained at home and dug in his own cellar or underneath his own wheat fields or in his own garden, instead of wretchedness, starvation and death by suicide in a strange land, he would have had acres of diamonds."
He stresses throughout his book the importance of looking within your own available resources for your opportunities. He demonstrates his belief with tales from the first oil well in Titusville, Pennsylvania, to the finding of gold in California. His is a strong message; before casting aside your resources, whatever they may be, be certain you have not overlooked the opportunities within.

Remember:
1. Plan for diversity. Do not be captive to only a few customers. Customer attrition is a way of business life. You will always need new customers. Plan to lose your best customer.
2. Welcome change—it will create opportunities for you not just problems.
3. Plan for product diversity. Business survival requires more than a single product or service. Plan each product's funeral. No successful product or service lasts forever.
4. Your success may lie within. Search deeply for "overlooked" possibilities.

Chapter 22
Partners and investors

Unless you plan on being the sole owner of your business, you will have others sharing in your success or failure. They can be partners or investors—silent or active; the right ones can be invaluable and the wrong ones can bring on your failure.

Hopefully, you will be able to be choosy, but be careful. There are glib characters who may see an opportunity for a quick gain at your expense. There are those who talk about work but are lazy and will let you do it all. Then there are those who will never be successful and you will find them a liability. If possible, with all the odds against your success, do not add to the pile with incompetent, lazy or dishonest associates.

When you are searching for money, it is tempting to say yes to the first person who sees merit in your proposition. Although you may be in desperate need of investors, do not jump at the first offer. Would you marry a stranger? Active partners and investors are similar to spouses in many ways. Your life and financial well being will be linked to their actions and behavior.

When you enter into a co-ownership arrangement, be certain there is an understanding of the roles of your new associates. Will they become corporate executives? Will they play an active role in management? Do they insist on being on your board of directors? Will they bring anything besides money to the company? How will authority and responsibility be shared? All of these questions need definitive answers when you establish your business, not later, when you have problems.

Should you have a partnership, corporation or other form of business?

Before you form your business, you need to select the form of your business: sole proprietorship, partnership, corporation or some variation allowed by your state. The first step in creating your business should include meetings with (1) your attorney on the benefits and downsides of incorporating your business or other ways to limit your personal liability and control your business and (2) your accountant to learn about the tax advantages and disadvantages of each alternative.

Sole proprietorship

As a sole proprietor you are naked. If you establish your business as a sole proprietorship, you may risk everything you own, even future earnings, as you are personally responsible for all business debts, taxes and other liabilities such as judgments. Unless you are starting a small business that requires little investment, little debt and has little chance of lawsuits, don't be a proprietor; it is a foolish and unnecessary risk.

Partnership

There are different kinds of partnership arrangements depending upon state laws. Each kind provides a different measure of protection again personal liability. However, the usual kind of partnership may expose you to the same risks that a sole proprietorship faces—even more so. Creditors and the bankruptcy court may go after the personal assets of each partner or just one partner. They will go after whomever has assets. Furthermore, if your partner obligates the partnership in any way, you may also be responsible. So, a partnership form of business organization may mean that you are doubling your risk. Obtain legal advice as to how certain special partnerships may limit your risk.

Incorporation and other entities to limit liability

If you follow only one suggestion in this book, follow this one: incorporate or form some type of entity that limits your personal liability for business debts and obligations (once your attorney and CPA have confirmed it's best for you)! In general, if you form a corporation, for example, and properly dot all the i's and cross the t's through the years, you will not have unlimited liability. In general, shareholders are not liable (i.e., they only have limited liability) beyond their investment in the business unless they sign personal guarantees or the corporation does not follow all the rules. However, you have no limited liability protection against the IRS or other taxing entities.

Pursuit of a partner

Unfortunately, an acquaintance of mine is in a business with a partner he detests. They agree on little. Even though they have been in business for thirty years, they still irritate each other and act like spiteful spouses. Their rocky relationship has cost them numerous opportunities over the years.

As you will discover, the personal chemistry among your co-owners is important to your peace of mind and the future success of your business. How well all the owners relate to each other will influence their collective harmony. As soon as you sell a piece of your business or join someone else's, you will find yourself in a complementary, compatible or a conflicting relationship. It is not to be entered into lightly.

I prefer a complementary one as it can be beneficial to have offsetting strengths and talents. These relationships usually work well because one person has what the other does not. For example, one may have administrative talents while the other is a whiz at selling. Hewlett-Packard was started with such a relationship. David Packard did the outside selling and Bill Hewlett handled the inside details.

If the relationship is compatible, it is workable. Compatible owners operate in harmony without using their energy on nonproductive disagreements. If they share mutual goals and approaches to these goals, there is less for them to disagree over. It is common sense that any business with stress-free owner relations has a better chance of success.

The least effective is the relationship that has deteriorated into conflict. It is not productive and drains each of energies better directed to the growth and success of the business. Such conflict can develop in numerous ways: a difference in goals, a difference in management style, a difference in ethics, a difference in people skills or a difference in business philosophy.

Investors and shareholders

There are "angels" who have money to invest, but most have stringent requirements your new business may not be able to meet. Some "angels" are willing to be silent and play no part in the management of your business; others insist on a role in the running of it. Some are professional management or venture capital companies that specialize in finding start-up companies with potential that they can orchestrate towards a future public stock offering. These firms are selective and reject most inquires. They favor the hi-tech sector with potentially large markets.

Finding investor money is difficult. Banks usually say no to start-ups. If they say yes, they will insist on a personal guarantee. As I have suggested, if you wish to sleep nights, you are wise to avoid such guarantees. Why risk all that you have?

You may wish to look at the classified ads of investors seeking investment opportunities. My experience with most such individuals is that they do not understand the problems of a start-up business. They become impatient and meddlesome. If you place an ad looking for money, expect curiosity seekers, opportunists and sleight-of-hand artists.

If you decide to ask friends and relatives (which may be your best source), I caution you against painting an overly optimistic future. If you fail and they lose their money, it may not be pleasant. A friend of mine lent his son a portion of his retirement nest egg to finance a business. It went bust. The loss was difficult for both—it strained their relationship for some time.

Investor expectations may affect your future relationship with your investor(s). They invest with you—leaving the safety of banks and expecting high rates of return and capital gains. You must make them realize that if they become unhappy and demand to cash out, you will not be able to write a check. Their money is, most likely, invested in equipment, inventory, customer credit or other assets and is not immediately available. Unlike a publicly-traded stock on one of the exchanges, your business is not a liquid investment. If you wish a good relationship, any person investing in your business should understand it is a long-term commitment, not a short-term opportunity.

Control may be another issue. Knowledgeable investors may shy away from a minority position in a small private company realizing that if performance is not to their liking, they will have little voice and little chance of liquidating their investment.

You may be asked to give up control. It will not be an easy decision. If it is the price you must pay to get investment capital, more than ever you will need legal advice to protect yourself. Trading a major portion of your control for money to launch your business is tricky. If you are successful you may feel later on that you sold too cheaply; on the other hand, if your business flounders, you may be removed from office. Giving up control in my opinion should only be a last resort.

"You can trust me"

To some, a handshake is a macho and romantic way of doing business. While such deal-making agreements are great theater, in real life they are risky and potentially troublesome. Misunderstandings and conflict between partners or among investors are common; disagreements and bad feelings can evolve from many circumstances. Even success creates as many partner problems as failure. Money affects our behavior. I believe most of us do not know how we will react to losing our money or the opportunity to grab a windfall.

Don't fall for the fantasy "we can trust each other." It is important to your company's health to stay away from "fuzzy" understandings. Clarity is necessary. The right time to develop an understanding that is clear and specific and addresses the problems that you can anticipate arising is when you start your business, not later. If you think discussing such issues will frighten off an investor, you are not being candid. Deal with the possibility of any misunderstanding at the start of the relationship not later. A misunderstanding may put you out of business.

Put it on paper

Conversations are easy to deny as well as misunderstand. Put your understanding of ownership and investor status in writing. If you can't, maybe your understanding of the proposed relationship is not clear. To help you formulate your thinking, ask yourself the following questions:

1. What do I want my associate(s) or investor(s) to do in my company?
2. How much reward do I feel they should be entitled to?
3. What will I do if I am not able to work harmoniously with the person(s)?
4. How will I deal with a problem of different expectations?
5. What will I do if they want their money back?

The answers should be the basis for any agreement with your fellow owners. Answering in detail will help everyone understand and clarify their expectations and relationship(s) with you. If you cannot agree to agree, what do you think will happen when money or disagreements are involved?

Splitting up: Plan for it

A prenuptial agreement is preplanning a possible divorce. Not always a pleasant task, but with half of all marriages ending in failure, it has become very common.

Why should you view your new business differently? With eight out of 10 new companies failing, agreements must acknowledge the possibility of the venture not surviving. A business split-up can be more complicated than most divorces. There are liabilities, creditors, cash flow, customers, employees, leases, taxes, inventory and a host of other issues to deal with. There is no "no fault" business divorce.

Without a properly written and executed agreement to guide you and your fellow owners, arguments, frustration, maneuvering and distrust can drag on until your business is destroyed.

There are many reasons why owners of a business may decide to part company. A serious illness, a family problem, a financial problem or a desire for new horizons are all situations you can not predict. Yet, all are possible. Take out some insurance. Plan for a business divorce by having a written "prenuptial" agreement. If your potential partners or investors balk, don't go into business with them. You will be wise to suspect their motivations and expectations. Without an agreement, you may expect problems and even the loss of your business.

What we're talking about here is a written buy-out agreement. Without a written buy-out agreement, the seller always wants more. A fair agreement contains a specific understanding of the terms and conditions of buying each other out, as well as an agreed-upon method of calculating the buy-out price.

A buy-out agreement protects all the owners. If any owner desires to sell they must be treated honestly and fairly, while at the same time protecting yourself and your company. If your venture has been successful, greed may be a strong motivation to your associates to cash out. Unless you determine well in advance the method to be used to calculate the buyout price, inflated perceptions of the value of the business can lead to difficult times. Disputes and emotionally-charged arguments resulting in inflated values can push a successful company into inflated debt and failure.

When your agreement is negotiated, here are a few provisions I suggest you review with your attorney:

1. Before any stock can be sold, should you (or the remaining investors) be given the right of first refusal to buy the stock? Otherwise, you will have no say in whom your new associates may be—a risky situation.

2. What should be the method of payment to the seller? It is rare that a company has enough cash reserves to finance a stockholder, all-cash buy-out. Usually, monthly payments over a period of years is more realistic.

3. Should the agreement include a stipulation prohibiting the departing stockholder from using company knowledge to affiliate with a competitor or to start a competing company?

4. Should the agreement prohibit the stock from being used as collateral (i.e, a guarantee) for any noncompany debt the stockholder may incur without approval from the board of directors? Otherwise, you may have some owners you may not want—the creditors who may take over the stock upon a default on the debt.

5. How will the buy-out price will be calculated? There are a number of approaches that you can use: book value, a multiple of earnings or sales or an appraisal. Your accountant and attorney should advise you on the best method for your company.

Buying your co-owners out or liquidating investor interests may not be important to you at this moment because these are future issues with a negative connotation and it may be tempting to push aside the possibility of ownership conflict. Don't! If you are uncomfortable discussing such arrangements and fearful of offending anyone, have your attorney do it. Whatever you do, don't be foolish about the future and think such problems only happen to others. You may be unpleasantly surprised.

Al & Mort: A Buyout Failure. Al and Mort found themselves out of work for the first time in twenty years. Their employer in upstate New York was now failing because of overseas competition. At the time of their dismissal, each received a small severance package to help tide them over.

A few weeks later, Mort asked Al if he would like to go into business with him. Mort told Al about a commercial property located on a highly traveled highway that was available and proposed they buy it and build a storage rental center. It would be the only center within 25 miles. Because the area was building up with apartments and condominiums, Mort was certain there would be a demand for short- and long-term storage rentals. Al agreed, but expressed his reluctance to remain in the North; however he did share Mort's optimism. Using their severance pay and savings, they incorporated, bought the lot and borrowed on the equity in their homes to build the center.

Mort's vision was correct. Within a few months after opening, only three spaces were vacant. It was a success. As partners they worked well together. Except for a part-time employee on busy Saturdays, they ran the center without outside help. It was an easy business for them. The biggest problem was the occasional deadbeat they had to chase for monthly rental fees. Beyond that, all went well. From the profits, they were able to take home a modest, but adequate income. They felt lucky.

After a few years, Al became bored. He grew restless waiting in the office for the occasional new customer. He wanted more action—office work was not something he enjoyed doing. He discussed his feelings with his spouse. Perhaps, she told him it was time to make the change and move to a warmer climate. If they sold their half of the business to Mort, they could pay off the mortgage on their home and head South with enough money to start a new life.

Al presented his decision to Mort. It was a bitter meeting. Mort became angry, feeling betrayed by Al's abrupt actions. After a few weeks of emotionally-charged discussions, they reached an agreement. Mort would borrow to buy Al's half using loans on the business pledging the business as collateral. The day Al signed over his ownership and picked up the check was the last contact the partners had with each other. It was not a friendly parting.

The burden of the debt was troublesome for Mort. Besides the payments of principal and interest, without Al, he had to hire employees. The fun and sense of accomplishment were gone for Mort. The parting left him bitter. Customers noticed the change and he was not pleasant to be around. Mort felt betrayed by his partner whom he had believed was his best friend.

Sensing an opportunity the following year, a group of local business persons decided to open a competing center. The impact was immediate. The new facility was offering lower rental rents with a more pleasant environment. It was not long before Mort's income declined. With the debt payments and a loss of business, a financial crisis was brewing. The more customers he lost, the more angry he became, blaming all his troubles on his former partner. Three years later, the bank foreclosed. The successful business became Mort's nightmare. Al walked away with the money and Mort got the debt.

Mort's nightmare did not need to happen. If there had been an understanding and an agreement explaining the possibility of parting company and provisions had been included to make the buy-out less burdensome to the one remaining owner, an equitable arrangement could have been crafted to protect everyone.

We can learn from Aristotle, the Greek teacher and intellectual who saw harmonious relationships as critical to well being. He concluded that successful "partnerships" are a basis of living well. Whom you select to be in business with is as important as selecting a business to be in.

Remember:
1. Talk to your attorney and accountant about whether a corporation or other type of entity will be best for you and your business for liability and tax reasons.
2. Partners can be permanent—don't jump at the first offer of money. Relationships can be complementary, compatible or conflicting. Misunderstandings come from no under standing.
3. Have a written plan if you split up. "Prenuptials" are necessary in business, too. A business break-up can be as emotionally draining as divorce. Inflated buy-out agreements can result in inflated debt.

Chapter 23
A second chance at success

If your business has deteriorated into insolvency, you may be thinking about calling it quits. You may be saying to yourself, "Anything is better than these angry phone calls and legal threats." You may be asking yourself, "Why did I ever start this nightmare?" In comparison, your past life style may have seemed calm and comfortable. Your family and friends are probably telling you to get out of it and get a job! You are undoubtedly feeling pressure from everyone: family, friends, creditors, employees, partners and tax collectors. It may be the worst time of your life.

Bankruptcy may look attractive to you. After all, you rationalize, business bankruptcies are common; there is no shame in it. But be careful, if you are "stressed out," you may not be thinking clearly. Unless your creditors are putting your business into involuntary bankruptcy, don't you volunteer it! Yes, a voluntary bankruptcy reorganization is a way out for some firms; however, many who ask for the protection of the court against actions by their creditors never emerge as an independent and healthy business. When you ask a judge to protect you, you have submitted your business to the will of a creditors' committee.

You may be president but the committee is your new "board of directors." You no longer have sole discretion over the matters of your business. You will be required to submit a financial plan specifying how you are going to run the business and pay your bills. You will find yourself with little control. If you fail to meet your new obligations, the committee can recommend to the judge that your business be declared bankrupt and its assets liquidated. I caution you about any eagerness to seek the court's protection—you will give up control and your business may never be yours again. There are better ways to keep it alive.

No one wants your business to fail. You don't, your investors and associates don't, your employees don't, your customers don't and your creditors definitely do not. A failed business brings losses to all, yet few lose in the long run if it stays alive. Your inner strengths, your talents and your persistence will determine if it makes it. The miracle must come from you.

The art of survival

Don't accept all debt obligations at face value. Most creditors will listen to proposals unless you have made past promises and ignored your commitments. It is not in the best interest of any people to whom you owe money to share in the meager pickings of your failed enterprise.

Find a way to settle

Even if you have managed to "manage" the business into insolvency with your liabilities exceeding your assets, few are eager to foreclose on you as they know they will not be paid in full. Your suppliers do not want to lose their money and a customer. Your bank may listen to a reasonable debt reduction program; a bad loan write-off or a foreclosure is not pleasant banking. Even the Internal Revenue Service may negotiate with you.

I hope you have not signed personal guarantees with any creditors. If you have, they may be able to take your personal assets as well as your business assets. A personal guarantee removes your leverage to negotiate. Creditors may ask you to sign guarantees as a condition of any settlement. Don't do it without first getting proper legal advice as to the consequences. In fact, don't sign any settlement agreement without first getting legal advice. Settlements do not assure your business will be successful; they only buy you time. Don't agree to any payment program hoping for a miracle. Be sure you can pay it. If for any reason you cannot honor these new commitments, you will find your creditors difficult to deal with. They will not have faith in you to keep your word or your ability to save your business.

Unfortunately, some creditors have a history of dealing with failing companies and they demand to be paid in full. The electric company, the telephone company, the water company, your insurance agency, your landlord and the tax collector have all heard many tales of woe from failing entrepreneurs. You will not get any sympathy from them.

Banks are tough; some will settle, while others will not. If you know you are getting into difficulty, see your loan officer. I suggest that you prepare a cash flow analysis and try to negotiate temporary arrangements to help you through the crisis. Don't ignore your bank and force them to call the loan and foreclose on any collateral you may have pledged. Loan officers know businesses can encounter problems meeting financial obligations, but they do not like surprises.

It is in the interest of your suppliers to keep you in business, otherwise they will lose their money as well as your future purchases. Assuming you have had good relations, most will "work" with you through your difficult times and be open to reasonable suggestions. Remember though, your negotiating strength is your implied threat of bankruptcy; be careful how you present it. No creditor wants that, unless they smell assets they can grab or there are some personal guarantees they can go after. They are aware, as unsecured creditors, of the dismal pay-out records of most business bankruptcies.

There are a variety of steps you can take to ease the financial pressure. First, try to reduce the amount you owe by returning any surplus or slow-moving inventory. If you are told it is the vendor's policy not to take back inventory, don't believe it. Faced with either bankruptcy or getting merchandise back, they will take their product. If returns are not an option and you need the supplier, arrange to buy C.O.D. with an offer of monthly small payments applied to the overdue outstanding balance. At least, they save a customer and recover their money. You can try asking for debt forgiveness with a pledge to remain a "cash customer." Sometimes that works. Some creditors will accept a partial cash settlement just to get your account off their books.

In 1991, I bought an interest in a near-bankrupt small company. At the time, the founder was discouraged and ready to return to his former employer. I made a deposit to his company's checking account to keep the doors open and began negotiating with the suppliers and other creditors. I made it clear to all if they balked at any reasonable settlement, I would let the company slide into bankruptcy. The majority were aware of the problems the company was experiencing and welcomed our offers. Within 60 days, we reduced the inventory by returning 60 percent of slow-moving and surplus inventory to suppliers and the accounts payable were also reduced by 60 percent.

With our debts more manageable, I tackled other problems. I negotiated a bailout of a repressive five-year lease and moved the company to smaller and cheaper facilities. I fired the accountant and attorney, who in my opinion contributed to the problem. And I made cash settlements with a few creditors with whom I did not plan on maintaining relationships. I looked everywhere to rid the company of losses and waste. And it worked.

Years ago I saw the benefits that forceful and focused negotiating strategies can accomplish during negotiations to buy an insolvent audio cassette duplicating company. Its suppliers refused to deal with it, the bank was threatening to take legal action and the IRS was demanding immediate payment of past due taxes. The financial reports showed three years of substantial losses and a negative net worth. The company was out of cash and ready to close its doors.

Our strategy was simple. We informed all the creditors that we would buy the company only if each creditor agreed to a debt forgiveness of 50 percent. Otherwise, we would walk away. It helped that these creditors knew and respected our company; all but one agreed. With the stroke of a pen the insolvent company's balance sheet became healthy. Within 90 days the company was profitable and soon became a major audio video tape duplicator in the Los Angeles market.

However you approach your problems, keep your promises.

Hang in there!
One reason for failing in business is quitting too soon. It is

prematurely succumbing to the pressures and problems brought on by the accumulation of losses and negative cash flow. Yet, when do you quit? Can you hang in there too long? It is a difficult personal decision. I have a rule of thumb which may help you to decide when to move on. If you are not investing more money or placing additional personal assets at risk, stay until you are forced out. When that time arrives, if it does, the decision has been made for you. And if you are not forced to shut your doors, you will have survived. Whether you can earn the money you may once have dreamed of is another issue.

According to your accountant and your financial reports, you may have lost your money, but it will only be a paper loss, unless you close the business. As long as you keep it going, there is the chance you will recover your money and more!

Staying afloat

At this stage of your crisis, you are left with these options: a reduction in expenses, an ultraconservative approach to your cash flow and a determination to boost sales.

Paring expenses is difficult to do. It is so much easier and exciting to expand. It is like the medieval practice of blood letting—painful, but vital to survival.

Don't look for the miraculous "big cut" because you will not find it. Look to every dollar you reduce in expenses as a new dollar in cash flow. For example, if you earn a 10 percent net profit, do you realize that a dollar saved is equal to the profit on sales of ten times that amount? Look everywhere for savings. Do you need the cellular telephone? Do you need the water cooler? Do you need the 800 number? Nothing should be off limits or thought to be unchangeable. Every expense you have must be questioned: Do you need it to stay in business?

Ask everyone for help. Ask for a reduction in rent. Ask your employees to take a pay cut. Ask anyone you owe or to whom you pay money—it is in their best interest that you survive. Don't spend a dollar you don't have to. Don't fall for the argument that it is just a few dollars and will not matter. To use a trite expression: "They all add up." How much do you have to cut back? You may have to cut enough to get rid of your losses.

Next, don't spend a single dollar that will not keep you in business. Your miserliness must be unrelenting. Don't celebrate anything. Don't reward yourself. Don't ever say you deserve some "treat"—the only thing you deserve is to save your business. It will require sacrifice and discipline and if you are not prepared to do so, quit now. If you still have credit with your suppliers, ask for the longest terms possible and give the shortest to your customers. Your limited cash is probably all that is keeping the business alive. It is precious.

Establish daily sales goals. Don't wait for "good things" to happen. Focus your positive thinking on selling. Remember Red Motley's expression, "Nothing happens until someone sells something." What could be more applicable?

Believe you will succeed

There are two critical moments when you must have faith in yourself and your business: when you start it and when it is in trouble. It is easy to be optimistic at the launch but not so when you are pressed in all directions with demands you cannot meet. Facing and overcoming business and financial adversity is not pleasant and not easy. There is no magic formula or painless shortcut except more money from investors or loans which probably are not forthcoming.

Instead, believe you will succeed and reflect on your initial feelings of optimism and excitement when you started your business. Focus on those feelings. Bolster your spirits by reading some of the positive thinking materials available in book stores and libraries. Do not let the possibility of defeat, defeat you. It is unfortunate that there are not self-help support groups to assist owners of failing and insolvent businesses. Such groups could be a refuge and source of inspiration offering hope and practical advice.

To turn your thoughts away from the fear of failing, I suggest that you ask yourself why you started your business. List your reasons—are they still valid? Ask yourself about your original expectations—are they still possible? Probe yourself, look to your inner-self for emotional strength to carry on with your efforts. If you feel overwhelmed with all your problems, put the total aside and deal with the pressures, the fears and the demands of others one day at a time. Big problems broken into small pieces look different. Without more financial resources you know your problems cannot be instantly dismissed, but accept them and realize that as your business gradually got into trouble, it may gradually get out of trouble. To do so it requires your faith in your abilities to overcome your problems and push your troubled business to survival, one problem and one day at a time. Try to keep in mind this famous Chinese proverb: "Man who says it cannot be done should not interrupt man doing it."

The sheriff and Adams Magnetics

If your business is in trouble and you see little chance of making it, let me leave you with hope by telling you about the darkest moment of Adams Magnetics.

Facing collapse in March of 1982, we closed our manufacturing plant, sold the equipment to pay some of our debt, arranged with a subcontractor to do our manufacturing and moved the remains of the company to a small office suite. At this time, my original stockholders washed their hands of me and the company, expecting bankruptcy. The remaining employees quit and I was alone with an answering machine.

My suppliers were suing for payment and I was just able to pay the telephone bill and office rent. The company was broke. I dreaded the mail, especially those certified letters; I knew they did not contain good news. I dreaded the phone calls; irate creditors are not always polite. I was forced to keep going, as I did not have the $3,000 my attorney wanted to file a bankruptcy petition.

I desperately sought hope. As I could not pay the bills and my new subcontractor insisted on controlling my accounts receivable (keeping most of the receipts), I was left with the option of going on the road selling. It helped and I was able to pick up enough business to cover the telephone and rent, but little was left to pay my debts.

Eventually, creditors grew tired of my promises and sued, obtaining judgments against my company. As I was unable to pay anyone anything and with no money for a lawyer, I accepted these dreaded court documents not knowing what to do.

All of my previous business experience and education did not prepare me for these emotions of failure. As a professor of business I was not setting an example of successful entrepreneurship. My feelings of self-confidence and self-worth evaporated. In a year I went from the excitement of a new business to desperation. It was awful.

I will never forget the Monday morning when the sheriff came to my office to tell me the assets of the company were to be auctioned to pay a major creditor. At that moment I believed the end had arrived. He looked around, saw the remaining few items of office furniture and said, "There is nothing here. I am going to suggest your creditors find some way of settling."

That was a turning point for me. As broke as Adams Magnetics was, I could not wash my hands of it. I had the choice of finding a way to stay in business or walking out the door. As much as I wanted to quit and put these problems behind me, I didn't do so—I felt an inner drive not to.

When my creditors realized there was no money, no assets of any value and my accounts receivable were controlled by my subcontractor, I was able to get agreements to settle for 10 to 30 cents on the dollar. Three years later, the old debt was gone and the business survived and has thrived.

Ironically, the sheriff kept me in business. I share this tale with you to offer encouragement that no matter how desperate your situation may be, there is always a glimmer of hope if you can outlast your problems and adversaries. Hold on to the thought that you do not lose your money until you close your doors.

Remember:
1. If at all possible, avoid any form of bankruptcy.
2. Avoid all personal guarantees.
3. Avoid quitting too soon. Many a turn-around miracle has happened.
4. Negotiate settlements—your business is worth more alive.
5. Your threat of bankruptcy is your strength.
6. You can survive if you cut your expenses, conserve cash and boost sales.
7. Never give up. Do not let defeat, defeat you. Believe you can succeed.
8. You have to close the doors to lose your money.

Chapter 24
A few positive words
from the author

Before putting this book away, carefully read this chapter (including my appendix on understanding financial statements) and I believe you will increase your chance of succeeding. I wish you such success as I want you to enjoy the feeling of starting and owning a profitable business just as I have. You will find it a wonderful sense of accomplishment that is possible with your efforts and determination. I wrote this book having experienced failure and success and I know there is no easy way to survive in business without hard work and discipline. Yes, luck and good fortune do help, but first you must learn to help yourself, acting with maturity and wisdom. If you do, fortune may follow. Remember:

Failure and personality
I believe a majority of start-up business failures is caused by the actions of the owners. To what extent these failures are due to the personality traits or characteristics and/or subconscious motivations of the founders are factors anyone considering risking their savings or borrowings to start a business should think about seriously.

Money

If you lack an understanding of money management, you may discover your ability to survive in business requires more than simple recordkeeping. You will need the discipline to work efficiently with limited funds and manage cash flow. You can fail in business if you have too much money; you will fail if you run out of money; and you may fail if you do not know you are losing money.

Leadership

Leadership in a start-up is not like that of a mature organization; it demands a sense of urgency and an "action" style quite different from the "process" style of established companies. It requires action such as increasing sales, acquiring customers, developing products and collecting money. Time is critical; the longer the losses continue, the closer to bankruptcy you are. Start-ups mandate action, not discussion.

Marketing

Are you sales-minded? Don't fall for the myth that salespersons are born not made. Sales training, motivation and your leadership skills are important to your survival. If you have any fear about selling, get over it. If your new business is going to survive, learn to sell your product or service without hesitating to ask for the order. To requote Red Motley, "Nothing happens until someone sells something." Promotion is essential—don't hide your business. Your potential customers must know you exist. Before you open your doors, you should have an understanding of your customers—who they are, where they are, how many you can sell to and how much you can sell to them.

Strategies for success

What is a strategy? It is an approach to a goal: your goal of
survival, your goal of a successful business venture that will
reward you with your definition of success. You need to follow a
set of strategies that will allow you to sidestep the potential
"traps" that can bring your new business to a tragic ending. But
staying out of "traps" is not enough; you need a strategy of
success, not just a business plan, but a set of guidelines similar
to a set of principles that will help keep you on your path to
success.

A final word

Let me leave you with the following comments. If you are
debating taking the plunge and going into business—and it is a
sound and fiscally conservative proposal—do it, but do not risk
everything unless you are young, perhaps in your twenties. And
if you do, don't worry; you have time to recover and even try it
again. However, if you are middle-aged, fifty or so, time is
against you if you fail—you may not recover your financial
health. To my middle-aged and senior friends, I say, be cautious,
careful and conservative. Old age and poverty are not an enjoy-
able lifestyle.

If you take the step to entrepreneurship, be prepared for the
struggle, the disappointment, the frustration and the ever-
present "Murphy's Law." If you make it, you look forward to
experiencing a wonderful sense of accomplishment and well-
being. Owning and running a successful and money-making
business is an exciting journey. You will find the hardship and
sacrifice worth it. Good luck!

Appendix
Traditional
financial statements

Information is vital to your business success. The more informed you are about the financial workings of your business, the more intelligent your decisions will be. There are two standard financial documents that indicate a business's financial condition and performance—the balance sheet and the income statement.

The balance sheet takes a snapshot of the business on a given day. It shows, for example, the assets (the plus side) and debts (the minus side) of the company on any given day (for example, December 31) and whether the owner(s) have a positive or negative balance in the business (assets less liabilities).

The second financial form, the income statement, shows profit or loss for a period of time (e.g., for the entire calendar year 2002). While, these reports are necessary for tax returns and shareholder information, if not properly understood, they can actually be misleading.

What your balance sheet does not tell you

A business is always changing. Cash is deposited, checks are written, merchandise is being shipped and received, old bills are paid, and new ones are received. The change is constant. But the balance sheet is a static report. It is a view of the financial condition of a company at one moment in time. It is a document that lists a company's assets and liabilities on a given date. It is a list of what your company owns expressed in dollars less what the company owes in dollars, with the difference being the owner's equity or net worth. As the company earns profits, the equity portion increases, whereas losses decrease the equity. If the equity is a minus amount, the company is insolvent.

The balance sheet (Table 7) has a common-sense structure to it. On the asset (plus) side, all items the company owns fall into two basic categories: (1) current or short-term and (2) fixed or long term.

Short-term or current assets include cash plus those items (such as inventory and accounts receivable) which should convert to cash in less than a year.

Fixed or long-term assets are such items as machinery, trucks, autos and buildings that are not usually convertible to cash in the normal course of doing business.

On the liability (minus) side, the amounts owed creditors are grouped into current and long-term categories the same way assets are. Current liabilities are debts that require payment normally within 30 days or less such as payroll taxes and bills from suppliers. Long-term liabilities are amounts owed over a longer period of time such as mortgages, bank notes, or auto payments. The left side of a balance sheet (current assets and long-term assets) always equals the right side of a balance sheet (current liabilities, long-term liabilities and owner's equity).

Table 7
An Example of a Balance Sheet

CURRENT ASSETS		CURRENT LIABILITIES	
Cash (checking account)	$5,000	Accounts Payable	$90,000
Accounts Receivable	$80,000	Taxes Payable	10,000
Inventory	$65,000		
TOTAL CURRENT ASSETS	$150,000	TOTAL CURRENT LIABILITIES	$100,000
LONG-TERM ASSETS		LONG-TERM LIABILITIES	
Equipment	$30,000	Debt on Equipment	$20,000
		OWNER'S EQUITY	$60,000
TOTAL ASSETS	$180,000	TOTAL LIABILITIES and EQUITY	$180,000

How is your balance sheet doing?
To determine the financial status of a business, credit managers, financial analysts, and others use various ratios and other calculations to analyze a company's balance sheet. The most common one is the "current ratio."

To calculate the current ratio, current assets are divided by current liabilities. The resulting ratio or fraction is a measure of a company's ability to pay its current bills.

On the balance sheet above, the current ratio is calculated as follows: first, add up the current assets (consisting of cash, accounts receivable and inventory) which total $150,000 and then divide that total by the current liabilities (consisting of accounts payable and taxes payable of $100,000). The resulting current ratio equals 1.50 ($150,000 divided by $100,000).

What does this mean? The ratio of 1.50 signifies that if all the inventory were sold (at what it cost the business) and all the money owed to the business were collected, the business would be able to pay its bills and have some money ($50,000) left over. Well-managed companies strive to achieve current ratios of two or three to one. When current assets are two or three times the amount of current liabilities, there is little difficulty in meeting the bills and those businesses enjoy excellent credit ratings and financial stability.

On the other hand, a ratio of less than one to one indicates the business is having a problem paying its bills. When current debts exceed current assets, there will be a cash shortage.

Net worth (equity) margin
Another important measurement is the ratio of owner's equity to the total debt structure. In our example, the total liability and equity figure of $180,000 includes only $60,000 as the owner's equity. This amount is a margin of safety. If it is wiped out due to losses or decline in asset values, the firm may become insolvent.

Numbers on balance sheets are based on certain assumptions, not absolute truths. It is important to note that the values on balance sheets are based on the assumption of collecting all the money customers owe the business and being able to sell all the inventory at the amount paid for it (not as the amount the inventory should sell for). As long as a company continues to do business as usual, these assumptions are useful but if a company is forced to liquidate, inventory will be sold at distress prices.

Assets as cash eaters

Your accounts receivable and inventory can tie up your money for a long time. When you send a supplier a check for inventory that is not selling but is instead accumulating dust, you are tying up money you'll probably need to pay other bills or the payroll.

Until a customer pays you, the cash you have spent to provide the product or service remains tied up in your accounts receivable. Slow-paying or non-paying customers rob you of the use of your money.

To fully understand a balance sheet, you must look at the condition of the assets, particularly accounts receivable and inventory. The actual condition of any firm may be hidden from you. What good is a million dollars of inventory if customers have little need for it? And what does $100,000 of accounts receivable really mean if $50,000 is really not collectable?

Do not accept balance sheets (and other financial statements) at face value

A few years ago I was part of a negotiating team analyzing a possible purchase of a small manufacturing company. Initially, we were thinking of making an offer of a considerable amount. Then we began to analyze the company's balance sheet. When we discovered that most of the inventory of raw materials and components was nearly worthless due to age and obsolescence, we reduced our offer. As it turned out, the investment paid off because of our revised lower offer. If we had accepted the balance sheet at face value as the former owners wished us to do, we would have paid way too much.

What your income statement should tell you

Income statements (Table 8) like balance sheets have a structure to them that is universally understood by accountants and the Internal Revenue Service. They have 4 major categories: sales, the cost of the product you sold, the expenses you incurred to sell the product and the remaining profit or loss. The financial information is arranged around two calculations. First, start with your sales or income and subtract the cost of the product or service you sell to determine your (gross) profit. From this gross profit, subtract the rest of your business expenses to calculate your profit or loss, leaving you a net profit or loss.

Table 8
An Example of an Income Statement For the Year 2002

Sales		$1,000,000
Less:	Cost of goods	750,000
	Gross profit	$ 250,000
Less:	Expenses	200,000
Profit before taxes		$ 50,000

Assume you sold a million dollars worth of merchandise in the year 2002, which cost you $750,000 or 75 percent of your sales. You are left with $250,000 or 25% of each dollar of sales to pay your expenses. If your expenses are $200,000, you will have a profit of $50,000 or 5% of each dollar of sales ($50,000 divided by $1 million in sales).

With only a nickel profit from each dollar a customer spends with you, there is little room for error. Another way of looking at these particular numbers is that it takes an extra $20 of sales to make one extra dollar of profit or to pay for one extra dollar of costs. I mention this to stress the importance of adopting sound and conservative financial management practices which are necessary for you to avoid losing your money. Depending upon who is your accountant, he or she may be more interested in your payroll taxes and income tax liability than your cash flow or "real" profitability. When your accountant constructs your income statement, it may be prepared solely with the objective of minimizing your tax liability. In my opinion, too many CPAs focus on the tax code and forget such business basics as cash flow, gross profit, inventory turnover and receivables turnover (see Chapter 5).

Index

About the Author

Dr. Paul E. Adams has taught entrepreneurship, management and marketing for over twenty years and has put his knowledge into practice by starting and operating a number of successful businesses.

He has also personally experienced the brink of near business failure and has learned the hard way how to avoid disaster.

Besides being an entrepreneur, Dr. Adams is Professor of Business Administration Emeritus at Ramapo College where he was a founding faculty member, the creator and founder of the college's business program. Adams has worked for large and small companies—all of which gives him a broad base of business experience. He holds an Ed.D. from the University of Sarasota, an MBA from Boston University and a BSBA Magna Cum Laude from the same institution.

In short, Adams is a veteran businessman and professor who can be trusted to show you the ropes in today's challenging marketplace.

(Just in case you're wondering, Paul Adams has not added book publishing to his entrepreneurial ventures—it's just a coincidence that Adams and Adams-Hall Publishing have the "Adams" name in common.)

To contact author Paul E. Adams or for additional information on *Fail-Proof Your Business*:

email: paul@pcsonline.com